THE UPPER ROOM

WHERE THE WORLD MEETS TO PRAY

Sarah Wilke
Publisher

INTERDENOMINATIONAL
INTERNATIONAL
INTERRACIAL

33 LANGUAGES
Multiple formats are available in some languages

The Upper Room
May–August 2015
Edited by Susan Hibbins

The Upper Room © BRF 2015
The Bible Reading Fellowship
15 The Chambers, Vineyard, Abingdon OX14 3FE
Tel: 01865 319700; Fax: 01865 319701
Email: enquiries@brf.org.uk
Website: www.brf.org.uk
BRF is a Registered Charity

ISBN 978 0 85746 131 5

Acknowledgments

Printed by Gutenberg Press, Tarxien, Malta

The Upper Room: how to use this book

The Upper Room is ideal in helping us spend a quiet time with God each day. Each daily entry is based on a passage of scripture, and is followed by a meditation and prayer. Each person who contributes a meditation to the magazine seeks to relate their experience of God in a way that will help those who use The Upper Room every day.

Here are some guidelines to help you make best use of The Upper Room:

1. Read the passage of Scripture. It is a good idea to read it more than once, in order to have a fuller understanding of what it is about and what you can learn from it.
2. Read the meditation. How does it relate to your own experience? Can you identify with what the writer has outlined from their own experience or understanding?
3. Pray the written prayer. Think about how you can use it to relate to people you know, or situations that need your prayers today.
4. Think about the contributor who has written the meditation. Some Upper Room users include this person in their prayers for the day.
5. Meditate on the 'Thought for the Day' and the 'Prayer Focus', perhaps using them again as the focus for prayer or direction for action.

Why is it important to have a daily quiet time? Many people will agree that it is the best way of keeping in touch every day with the God who sustains us, and who sends us out to do his will and show his love to the people we encounter each day. Meeting with God in this way reassures us of his presence with us, helps us to discern his will for us and makes us part of his worldwide family of Christian people through our prayers.

I hope that you will be encouraged as you use the magazine regularly as part of your daily devotions, and that God will richly bless you as you read his word and seek to learn more about him.

Susan Hibbins
UK Editor

In Times of/For Help with . . .

Below is a list of entries in this copy of *The Upper Room* relating to situations or emotions with which we may need help:

Rethinking What's Possible

'Then Jesus answered her, "Woman, great is your faith! Let it be done for you as you wish"' (Matthew 15:28, NRSV).

The Canaanite woman approached Jesus and begged him to heal her daughter, but Jesus dismissed her. He was sent, he told her, to minister only to his own faith. Yet the woman wouldn't take 'no' for an answer. 'Lord, help me,' she insisted. He rebuffed her, saying, 'It is not fair to take the children's food and throw it to the dogs.' She responded with, 'Yes, Lord, yet even the dogs eat the crumbs that fall from their masters' table.' Hearing that, Jesus had a change of heart and healed the girl.

Can you imagine arguing with Jesus? Rarely in the Gospels does he get anything but the last word, but here, the woman moved him to shift his thinking. She seemed to see in Jesus even more than he thought was possible, and her words inspired him to act.

I write this as I complete my fifth year as publisher of *The Upper Room*, and I can't help but be amazed by the journey that has taken me to this place. Almost 30 years ago, I began as an inner-city missionary, called to serve people in so much need. Through twists and turns that I couldn't have imagined then, I now have the privilege of leading a worldwide prayer movement. Along the way people—family, friends, mentors, pastors—helped me to see more in me than I thought possible. I also came to see how need—including spiritual need—comes in many desperate forms. Though much in my work has changed, I still feel I am answering my original call. And now, as I look to the future, I thank God for continuing to show me new possibilities.

Sarah Wilke
Publisher

More than seven years ago, two North American Methodist women, one a paediatrician, came to Honduras on a medical mission trip. They felt God's call to live among the poor and devoted themselves to evangelism and prayer. Inspired primarily by Christ, and also by the Benedictine and Quaker traditions, they made habits with their own hands and went to live on the north coast of Honduras, eleven hours from Tegucigalpa.

For more than four years, Faith and Joy have lived in a small wooden house in complete poverty and away from civilisation. They call this humble house their monastery. Sister Joy cares for the sick and together with Faith visits and shares the gospel. But what the two women do best is pray, and they use El Aposento Alto (The Upper Room) for that.

Every two months I send them 15 copies that they use for personal prayer and to teach others to pray. It's difficult to send the copies to them since there is no postal service where they live. So I send the copies to the town of Tocoa, about eight hours by car from their home. Then a Methodist pastor collects them and drives his motorcycle to deliver the copies to a Methodist church in a rural village two hours from where the women live. Every two months, Faith and Joy take a long walk to pick up their copies of El Aposento Alto.

In June 2013, I was able to visit them in person. Their 'monastery' is a wooden room with a small woodstove to the side. There I found a small library that had several issues of El Aposento Alto and a few Bibles and hymn books. What I noticed most about these two sisters is that despite the limitations, they are always smiling and serving the Lord with faith and joy.

Today, I would like to invite you to pray together for these and other missionaries and their ministries around the world.

Revd Juan Guerrero
Central America Distributor

The Editor writes...

What do you think about angels? The Bible is full of them. They act as messengers from God, bringing the alarming but joyful news to Mary that she would become the mother of Jesus; filling the sky with wonder and light on the night of Jesus' birth. They also warn of danger, making sure that Joseph took his new family away to Egypt before Herod's soldiers arrived to murder the babies of Bethlehem. After his struggle with hunger and temptation in the desert angels minister to Jesus, and after his cruci-fixion, it is an angel who asks the women in the garden, 'Why do you look for the living among the dead?' (Luke 24:5, NIV).

In the Old Testament Abraham, at the oaks of Mamre, 'entertained angels unawares'. Jacob, alone and comfortless after leaving home, dreams of angels passing to and fro between heaven and earth. Daniel is protected from the lions by an angel of God. When Elijah is afraid and depressed he flees into the wilderness, lies down under a broom bush and wants to die. It is an angel who comes to him, comforts him and tells him to eat so that he might regain his strength (1 Kings 19:3–9).

How do these accounts fit into our 21st-century lives? Are they relevant to us? Do angels still minister to people today in the same way as they do in the Bible? Before you say no, think for a moment. What about that time when a complete stranger helped you to find your way in an unfamiliar city? Do you remember the conversation you had with someone on a train which helped you make sense of something which was troubling you? Or the day when you were feeling afraid, and someone's encouraging smile or word made you feel better? These might not be angels in the sky, or the winged seraphs of Christmas cards, but they can be God's messengers still, who 'guard us in all [our] ways' (Psalm 91:11).

Susan Hibbins
Editor of the UK edition

The Bible readings are selected with great care, and we urge you to include the suggested reading in your devotional time.

Proclaiming Christ in Love

Read John 13:31–35
'By this everyone will know that you are my disciples, if you love one another.'
John 13:35 (NIV)

Recently, a young missionary couple visited us. Jeff had been the tall, skinny kid who played football down the street. As he grew up, he felt God calling him into mission work. Now he and his wife, Channy, were going to Cambodia, a country with a tiny Christian population, to spread the good news of Christ.

As Jeff talked with us about his work, we could see his passion for these people God loves. Jeff offers free English lessons, using the Bible as one of his texts. He and Channy have begun youth groups, and he recently started a sports club. In a video made by a fellow missionary, young Cambodian men and women testified that they treasure Jeff's classes because he respects them and doesn't shame them for wrong answers. They feel loved. As a result of their relationship with Jeff and Channy, some have decided to follow Christ.

We can't all be missionaries in foreign lands. However, we can send a card of encouragement, run an errand for an elderly neighbour or listen to someone who is in pain. Through acts of love, we show others the love of God.

Prayer: *Dear God, thank you for the love you have shown us. May we lead others to you through the love we show them. Amen*

Thought for the day: Love lights the path to God.

Susan Thogerson Maas (Oregon, US)

God's Guidance

Read Joshua 3:1–5
The officers commanded, 'When you see the ark of the covenant of the Lord your God being carried by the Levitical priests… Follow it.'
Joshua 3:3 (NRSV)

After a wonderful family outing, I was listening to my phone messages and heard an urgent message from the hospital. 'Call the hospital immediately!' the voice said. My hands trembled as I dialled the numbers, dreading what I might hear. The message was that my father had passed away. I was terrified. I couldn't imagine my life without him. Dad was always there, always providing guidance. Now he was gone.

Joshua and the Israelites also needed guidance when they were faced with conquering the land of Canaan. God promised that if they followed the ark (followed him), he would lead them. They followed the ark, and God led them right through the Jordan River to victory in the battle over Jericho.

God's promise to guide our steps holds true for us today. If we look to God, we will know the way we should go, the way we should live. When my father passed away, I didn't know how to go on with life, but I kept praying and kept reading the Bible, allowing the Holy Spirit to direct my thoughts and actions, one day at a time.

Prayer: *Dear Lord, when we don't know what to do, what to think or what to say, help us look to your word and trust you to show us the way. Amen*

Thought for the day: Through prayer and reading scripture, we receive God's guidance.

John Bagdanov (California, US)

The Door to Life

Read John 10:1–11

Jesus said, 'I came so that they could have life—indeed, so that they could live life to the fullest.'
John 10:10 (CEB)

On two occasions my wife and I have visited the fascinating city of Florence, Italy as part of a tour group. We marvelled at the beauty and the wonderful, intricate craftsmanship of the bronze gates to the baptistery of the magnificent cathedral. Michelangelo described these biblical scenes as worthy to grace the entrance to Paradise.

However, I was disappointed to learn that had we been able to enter through those doors, we would have found ourselves in a huge room lavishly decorated on the floor, walls and ceiling—an inspiring spectacle. If only we had been given the opportunity to see it!

In a similar way, there are those who look at Jesus, who said, 'I am the gate', and are greatly impressed, marvelling at his life, his teaching and his attitude toward people. But then they fail to go beyond this discovery and never know the wonder of a personal relationship with Jesus. This experience can offer a whole new meaning and purpose to life. It is certainly good to know of Jesus; but we miss so much if we fail to know him as Saviour and companion in our daily lives.

Prayer: *Dear Lord, walk with us this day so that our lives show others our relationship with you and they may be encouraged to learn of you. Amen*

Thought for the day: Life at its best can become a reality as Jesus shares our way.

Bill Willis (New South Wales, Australia)

A Wake-up Call

Read Matthew 11:28–30
Your word is a lamp to my feet and a light to my path.
Psalm 119:105 (NRSV)

Just lately life had been tiring, pressured and stressful; my time in study and prayer had been limited. One morning when I was catching up on my meditations from *The Upper Room*, I realised I had just read a Bible passage and didn't recognise key people in it or what had happened in the story.

It was a wake-up call. How was my relationship with God going to be strong and healthy if I was only snatching minutes with him here and there? As I pondered this I felt the Holy Spirit telling me that depth, time and discipline in study was needed, and if I did this I would grow, deepen and reconnect with the Lord.

In turning back and spending time with Jesus, I've been blessed to find that he has uplifted, guided and strengthened me.

Prayer: *Loving heavenly Father, thank you that when we are weary and worn out, you want us to turn to you for comfort and rest. In Jesus' name we pray. Amen*

Thought for the day: I will make the time to nurture my relationship with Jesus.

Mandy Slade (Somerset, England)

God Still Loves

Read Psalm 139:2–12

If I take the wings of the morning and settle at the farthest limits of the sea, even there your hand shall lead me, and your right hand shall hold me fast.

Psalm 139:9–10 (NRSV)

Sadie, our six-month-old black Labrador puppy, has more energy than I have and can run faster than I can. The other day, she got away from me and raced off. I could not outrun her, so I walked after her. Sadie led me on a wild-goose chase through our neighbourhood. She kept looking back and changing direction for some 20 minutes as I steadily followed.

Finally Sadie ran into a corner and could not escape me. So she came back to me with a look in her eyes that said, 'I'm sorry. Do you still love me?' I just hooked the lead on Sadie's collar and stroked her head, and together we walked back home.

God's love is upon us and is pursuing us—wooing us even before we are aware of it and all throughout our lives. As the apostle Paul put it, 'While we were still sinners, Christ died for us' (Romans 5:8, NIV). I can run from God, and have on many occasions, yet he still lovingly, patiently pursues me until I run into a corner and come back asking, 'Do you still love me?' God's answer is always 'Yes.'

Prayer: *Dear Father, thank you for staying close to us even when we wander from you. Amen*

Thought for the day: God always welcomes us back.

Tim Burleson (South Carolina, US)

Praying Continuously

Read Luke 18:1–6

Pray without ceasing.
1 Thessalonians 5:17 (NRSV)

My son is in the US Army, stationed overseas. He usually writes once a month, updating me about what he is doing. Each time I receive a letter or phone call, I am so grateful to hear that he is safe and sound. His happy tone always brings a wave of relief to me. At one point, however, five months passed without a word or response to my voicemails, text messages or letters. Even though I told myself, 'No news is good news', I couldn't help worrying about him. Every day I prayed, asking God to keep my son safe and to protect and guide him.

When my son telephoned on Mother's Day, I could not believe the intensity of my happiness and gratitude for that gift. At that moment, the scene between the prodigal son and his father came to life in my heart: 'While he was still far off, his father saw him and… ran and put his arms around him and kissed him' (Luke 15:20). I also felt tremendous gratitude for the answer to my prayers. But I am also grateful for the five months of waiting because that time of not knowing deepened my faith in God. Talking with God every day helped me overcome my fear and calmed my spirit.

Prayer: *Dear God, thank you for the opportunity to help us grow in faith and love. Remind us that prayer helps us to build and nurture our relationship with you. In Jesus' name. Amen*

Thought for the day: Like any loving parent, God wants to hear from us.

Phyllis Durante (Hawaii, US)

PRAYER FOCUS: PARENTS OF THOSE SERVING IN THE ARMED FORCES   13

Controlling Our Thoughts

Read Philippians 4:4–9

The mind governed by the flesh is death, but the mind governed by the Spirit is life and peace.

Romans 8:6 (NIV)

When I wake up long before my alarm clock goes off, I lie in bed and tell myself to go back to sleep. If I stay awake too long, my mind begins to race, my thoughts slip out of control and anxiety sets in. In the darkness I am beset by guilt, shame, regret and a host of other negative thoughts and emotions.

Fortunately, the Holy Spirit is beside me, encouraging me to shift my attention to thoughts of God. If I repeat words of thankfulness and praise, the Holy Spirit lifts me out of despair and leads me to a line of scripture or a devotional reading that is what I need to hear. When I have I finished reading, I write down my troubles and turn them over to God. In this way I find relief and a sense of peace.

God gives us many choices. The choices we make about what to think shape our self-image, our personality, our view of the world and our way of dealing with life's difficulties. The Holy Spirit is our source of comfort and peace and works with us to control our thoughts.

Prayer: *Dear God, help us to control our thoughts. Remove thoughts of despair and anxiety and fill our hearts with your peace, joy and love. Amen*

Thought for the day: God's love can overcome my despair.

Keith G. Williams (Alabama, US)

A Starting Point

Read James 5:13–18

The prayer of a righteous person is powerful and effective.
James 5:16 (NIV)

I work as a writer for a mission organisation. One morning my supervisor handed me a letter, saying, 'I'd like you to answer this because you write such good letters.' The letter—from a woman named Doris—consisted of several paragraphs requesting prayer for her macular degeneration, a devastating eye ailment. I prayed for Doris and also asked God to give me the words to respond to her letter. In my letter, I assured Doris that we had prayed for her and told her a little about my work. Then I asked her to pray for my husband, who is disabled from a stroke.

Several weeks later, a letter arrived from Doris—two pages, neatly written and cheerful. 'Your letter put a smile on my face,' she wrote. 'By all means, I'd be honoured to pray for your husband.' She wrote that having turned 93, she had been telling God, 'It is time for you to take me home.' Then she continued, 'But by the prayer requests I'm getting, the Lord seems to be saying, "Not yet."'

Doris's letter reminded me that when we think there's nothing we can do for God's kingdom, we can pray. Prayer isn't a last resort; it's a starting point.

Prayer: *Loving Father, thank you for allowing us to bring you our petitions and to pray for others. Amen*

Thought for the day: We all have work we can do for the Lord—prayer.

Janet Seever (Alberta, Canada)

Speeding Ticket

Read Romans 3:9–25

[God our Saviour] saved us, not because of any works of righteousness that we had done, but according to his mercy, through the water of rebirth and renewal by the Holy Spirit.

Titus 3:5 (NRSV)

When I was young I was driving through town when a sudden flash of blue light and the crisp, piercing sound of a siren interrupted the evening. Suddenly, I was being pulled over by a local police officer who booked me for speeding. When it was time to appear in court, I sat in the courtroom and contemplated how I would answer the officer's charge. I knew I was innocent of speeding, but I was guilty of carelessly driving through a red light.

When the time came, I stood before the judge and asked for leniency. He didn't dismiss the charge, but he drastically reduced the penalties, freeing me to continue enjoying the privilege of driving and the summer money I had earned.

When I think about this incident, I am reminded of how foolish it would be for us to argue with God that we are innocent of a particular sin, knowing how guilty we are of so many others. Wouldn't it be better for us all to ask for God's mercy and the freedom to enjoy the privilege of relationship and the joy of life everlasting?

Prayer: *Loving God, thank you for your mercy and grace. Help us daily to confess our sins and receive your forgiveness. Amen*

Thought for the day: God is merciful and hears my cries for grace.

Cassius Rhue (South Carolina, US)

A Spiritual Breakfast

Read Luke 18:15–17

Start children off on the way they should go, and even when they are old they will not turn from it.
Proverbs 22:6 (NIV)

My mother was a beautician and worked hard at her job. She loved to sleep, probably because of the long hard hours she put in, but she got up early every day to make sure we had breakfast. She also fed us with God's word. The first thing we did after coming downstairs was to listen to the reading of *The Upper Room*. Leaning on my mother's arm, I mostly slept as she read aloud the meditations. Often she would shake her arm to wake me and say, 'Did you understand that?' or 'God is just so good!' and I would always say, 'Yeah.' She knew I had been asleep, but she kept telling me about the importance of a relationship with God. Even though I missed most of her words, she still sacrificed her own sleep to ensure that I started the day hearing God's word.

After leaving home, I didn't give God much thought. I would pray for help when I was in trouble, but in general I just trudged on through life. I was 45 when I finally gave myself to God. A lot of people were involved in helping me turn my life around. And even though my mother was no longer alive, her spiritual nurture was at the core of my acceptance of Jesus as my Lord. I am grateful that God gave me such a faithful and loving mother.

Prayer: *Dear Lord, help us be your faithful witnesses today. Give us the wisdom to know how to show your love to those who don't yet know you. Amen*

Thought for the day: I can keep speaking for God, even when it seems as if no one is listening.

Janice D. Denton (Tennessee, US)

Password Prayers

Read 2 Thessalonians 1:11–12

We always pray for you.
2 Thessalonians 1:11 (NRSV)

Every month or so, a message appears on our computer screens at work: 'Your password has expired. Change it now.' Changing our passwords routinely is a way of safeguarding access to the computer network and to confidential information on it. However, coming up with a new password every 50 days and remembering it can be a challenge.

Most of us have devised a system to help us create memorable passwords. I have settled on the practice of letting my passwords remind me of people or situations I want to remember in prayer. As I enter the password and wait for the computer to come to life, I have at least a moment to call to mind a person or situation and pray. Over the last several years, I have password-prayed for my wife; for our daughters and their partners; for faith, hope and love; and for various events in my life.

This simple practice has become an important way for me to remember to pray for people or situations in my life.

Prayer: *Gracious Lord, in your mercy you are always present with us. Help us remember to bring to you the people and concerns that matter most to us. Amen*

Thought for the day: What we pray for shapes the people we will become.

William W. Barnard Jr (Ohio, US)

God is Our Rock

Read Psalm 18:1–4, 16

Turn your ear to me, come quickly to my rescue; be my rock of refuge, a strong fortress to save me.
Psalm 31:2 (NIV)

I look forward to the weekly Multiple Sclerosis water exercise class. My friends and I exercise while standing in the water, holding on to the solid edge of the pool.

One day there wasn't room along the edge, so I slowly waded over to hold on to the rope that marked off a lap lane. I started out fine with leg lifts until I suddenly got dizzy and lost my balance. I started flailing, and because the rope provided no sturdy support, I sank under the water. The instructor jumped in and rescued me and made me promise to hold on to the edge of the pool from then on.

That day at the pool I wasn't able to yell for help as I went under the water. In the same way, sometimes we aren't able or are too stubborn to call on God for help, but he knows when we need help. How many times has God held each of us up, whether physically, emotionally or spiritually, when we were sinking? God is our rock upon whom we can depend.

Prayer: *God of all power, you are our rock and strong fortress. We thank you that we can count on you to rescue us in our times of distress. Amen*

Thought for the day: When the waters of life overwhelm us, we can depend on God.

Sue Carloni (Wisconsin, US)

Son of Encouragement

Read 1 Peter 5:7–12

There was a Levite, a native of Cyprus, Joseph, to whom the apostles gave the name Barnabas (which means 'son of encouragement').
Acts 4:36 (NRSV)

During my formative years, my mum was my 'Barnabas', my encourager. As a woman of faith and prayer, she inspired me to seek God's will. When I told her of my call to pastoral ministry, she encouraged me to go to college and get an education. Forty-three years later, I'm still a minister.

Throughout my ministry God has been my ultimate encourager. When I am hurting, he listens as I pour out my heart in prayer. When I am discouraged, his word in the Bible inspires and challenges me. When I am frightened by the world's turbulence, God comforts me by sending the Holy Spirit to speak words of peace, and sends me friends who share words of hope.

We can follow God's example and be encouragers ourselves. When people are hurting we can listen with compassion instead of criticism or judgement. When others need to be encouraged, we can use scripture to console them and lift up their spirits. As the world swirls around them through tragedy, we can come alongside them and simply be present with them.

As the son of an encouraging mother, I am striving to be a son of encouragement like Barnabas was.

Prayer: *Dear God, encourage us so that we may encourage others. In Jesus' name we pray. Amen*

Thought for the day: Today I will look for opportunities to encourage others.

Derl G. Keefer (Michigan, US)

With All My Heart

Read Deuteronomy 6:1–9

Honour the Lord with thy substance, and with the firstfruits of all thine increase.
Proverbs 3:9 (KJV)

Growing up in a Christian family, I learned to give a tithe, as the Bible teaches. So with my first working income I was glad to tithe to the church.

Over the years, my income has increased. But the necessities of life have also increased, and as a result, I have sometimes forgotten to give a tithe. No, more precisely, I've avoided giving. I pray, 'Lord, forgive me; I can't give a tithe this month. Many needs use up my tithe. I hope I can give the tithe next month.' I hope God understands.

During one period, I found myself deferring my giving every month. I delayed tithing a first, second, third, fourth time—until one day, I heard a sermon that challenged me. The pastor said, 'Serving the Lord must be done with sincerity. If today we are sincere, then even if we struggle, serving will not be a burden.' The pastor offered as an example the many Christians who go to Sunday worship not with sincerity but as a routine. I realised that often I attend church out of a sense of obligation, and I do not tithe with a sincere heart. I want to serve God with all my heart.

Prayer: *Dear God, thank you for your blessing. Teach us to bless your church through our gifts. Amen*

Thought for the day: All that we do, we do for God.

Selly Miarani (Jakarta, Indonesia)

Releasing Potential

Read Galatians 3:13–14

For freedom Christ has set us free. Stand firm, therefore, and do not submit again to a yoke of slavery.
Galatians 5:1 (NRSV)

As a runner I know that flexibility is an important factor in performance. Not only does it make running easier but it determines how much strength I can draw from my muscles.

A coach recently informed me that my legs were only performing at 80 per cent of their capacity due to the tightness of my hamstrings. I began to stretch regularly and a few weeks later I was feeling much more supple and hoping to see an improvement when I ran.

However, on race day my time remained the same. I was puzzled but later realised that although I had the potential for greater movement I was still running as though my legs were restricted. When I made a conscious effort to lengthen my stride I found I could do so quite easily. All that potential was waiting to be released but I had not taken advantage of it; I had become accustomed to a set way of running.

We have been set free by Jesus, but we can easily become trapped in our comfortable way of life. To fully appreciate the potential he has placed in us, we need to step out in faith and discover our true capabilities.

Prayer: *Father, thank you that we have been set free. May we realise our true potential and use the gifts you have given us in your service. Amen*

Thought for the day: Jesus has set us free to live a new life in him.

Adam Pope (Northamptonshire, England)

The Big Picture

Read Jeremiah 29:11–13

Trust in the Lord with all your heart and lean not on your own under-standing.
Proverbs 3:5 (NIV)

Many years ago I was sitting on a small boat deck at a youth camp. I had been having a bad day; everything seemed to go wrong. Feeling sad, I looked down the river. The sun was just setting, and it caused a reflection of the trees in such a way that it looked as if the river ended there. However, having been down the river many times, I knew that after turning at an almost 90-degree angle, the river did continue beyond that point.

This experience reminded me of the many times in life that we feel we have reached a dead end in a situation—whether in a job, a relationship or any situation that makes us feel as if our path is leading nowhere. During times like these it helps to remember that God knows what lies ahead. He can see the whole river and knows that just around the bend lies something better. So when it looks as if life is not leading anywhere, we can trust God and then persevere around that bend in the river.

Prayer: *Dear heavenly Father, when we feel uncertain of the way ahead, help us to trust in you—knowing that your will for our lives is much better than we can ever hope or imagine. Amen*

Thought for the day: God sees the big picture.

Lia Evans (South Australia, Australia)

Ascension: Gift from the Father

Read Acts 1:1–11

Jesus said, 'I tell you the truth; it is to your advantage that I go away, for if I do not go away, the Advocate will not come to you; but if I go, I will send him to you.'
John 16:7 (NRSV)

My father was in the army and frequently travelled abroad for long periods of time. We missed him, but there was something we looked forward to when he returned: the reunion and his presence in our lives again. We would hug him and he would always give each one of us a gift, carefully wrapped, which we would tear into joyfully.

Ascension Sunday celebrates the gift that Jesus sent back to us after he ascended into heaven. John called it the 'Advocate' and Luke refers to it as 'power' from the Holy Spirit. Two aspects of this gift are somewhat like my father's return home. First, the Holy Spirit is the presence of God in our lives. Secondly, we can receive with joy the gift of divine power. It is not the power to dominate or control but the power for witnessing and service.

Prayer: *Dear Lord, help us to realise the gift that you have given to us and use it to bring Christ to others. In Jesus' name. Amen*

Thought for the day: God has given us the gift of the Holy Spirit and divine power to serve others.

Edward Kelly, Jr (Iowa, US)

God Pleaser

Read 1 Samuel 16:1–12

The Lord said to Samuel… 'People look at the outward appearance, but the Lord looks at the heart.'
1 Samuel 16:7 (NIV)

For many years, I sought people's approval by paying attention to the image in the mirror—how I looked and what I wore. I wanted to do my best to please my parents, employers and friends. Burdened by this quest for acceptance, I never found lasting contentment. My need for affirmation led to unrealistic expectations and broken relationships.

In the depths of despair, I cried out to God. The moment I said his name, I felt the warmth of divine love and wondered how the God of the universe could love even me. One day, as I tried to find my way back to God by reading the story of David, 1 Samuel 16:7 helped me to realise that God was not concerned about my appearance or performance but about what was in my heart.

I began to read the Bible with a new passion and learned ways I might please God instead of people. When I planned my days, I left time open to extend a helping hand or to share a smile or an encouraging word with someone in need. I gradually moved from a self-centred to a God-centred way of living and discovered a life's purpose that wasn't based on what I could earn but on what I could contribute.

Prayer: *Thank you, Lord, for your love and acceptance and for the opportunity to tell others what you have done. Amen*

Thought for the day: God looks past my appearance and abilities and into my heart.

Sue Tornai (California, US)

Ordinary Jars

Read John 2:1–11

The steward called the bridegroom and said to him, 'Everyone serves the good wine first, and then the inferior wine after the guests have become drunk. But you have kept the good wine until now.'
John 2:9–10 (NRSV)

When Jesus performed his first miracle at the wedding in Cana, he did not request special, priceless vessels. Jesus called simply for the ordinary, everyday water jars made of clay that could be found in every home and public building. From these commonplace vessels, the stewards surprised the wedding guests by pouring out the best wine that had been served that day.

In his ministry, Jesus continually turned society's expectations upside down. He chose to eat and pray with women and tax collectors. He fed a multitude with five loaves and two fish. And Jesus chose ordinary jars of clay—sinners like you and me—in which to pour the priceless gift of his love.

Like the stewards at the wedding at Cana who poured the best wine, we can pour out the love that Jesus has put in us so that many may be served and satisfied.

Prayer: *Loving God, make us stewards of your love that all those who touch our lives may be served and never thirst again. In Jesus' name we pray. Amen*

Thought for the day: God is ready to fill us with love to share with others.

Keith Honeyman (Western Cape, South Africa)

Granny's Girl

Read Romans 8:14–17
See what great love the Father has lavished on us, that we should be called children of God!
1 John 3:1 (NIV)

Recently my husband and I were shopping in a shoe shop when a four-year-old girl and her grandmother appeared. The child looked at me with the happiest smile you can imagine. I commented on the small shoe box that she held, and she eagerly showed me her new pink trainers. After our conversation, the girl took her grandmother's hand, and they began walking away. Then the child turned, looked back, and said proudly, 'I'm Granny's girl!'

How proud that little girl was of her new shoes, holding them close to her heart! But it was evident by the expression on her face and assurance in her words that her greatest joy was her loving relationship with her grandmother.

I was reminded of the many Bible verses in which God expresses a yearning for a loving relationship with us. How many of us are as sure of who we are and whose we are as that child was, and how often do we joyously proclaim it to others, even to passing strangers? For Christians this can be as spontaneous as a child expressing love for her grandmother. And so I proclaim with all the joyfulness and thankfulness of my heart, 'I am God's child—today and for ever!'

Prayer: *O God, may we always be proud and eager to tell the world that we are your beloved children. Amen*

Thought for the day: I am God's child—today and for ever!

Norma Hubbard (Mississippi, US)

Beginning the Day

Read Psalm 57:1–11

Awake, my soul! Awake, O harp and lyre! I will awake the dawn.
Psalm 57:8 (NRSV)

Contestants on a popular television show were asked to answer the question, 'How do people begin the day?' The number one answer drawn from a survey was 'with prayer'. I want to start my day with prayer. Before washing my face, shaving, eating breakfast, watching the news on television and setting out on the day's tasks, I want to spend time with the Lord.

I know that 'one does not live by bread alone, but by every word that comes from the mouth of God' (Matthew 4:4), so each morning I dip into the word of God in the Bible. I pray for myself and my needs. I intercede for others as the Holy Spirit moves me. Often, I say the Lord's Prayer. As I pray, I remember that God is my heavenly Father. I ask for sustenance, forgiveness and deliverance. I pray that above all, God may be glorified. Starting my day in this way helps me to put my faith first and to keep my focus on God all day long.

Prayer: *Our Father which art in heaven, Hallowed be thy name. Thy kingdom come, Thy will be done in earth, as it is in heaven. Give us this day our daily bread. And forgive us our debts, as we forgive our debtors. And lead us not into temptation, but deliver us from evil: For thine is the kingdom, and the power, and the glory, for ever.* Amen*

Thought for the day: Today I will begin my day with God.

Ted De Hass (Iowa, US)

Love Tracks

Read 2 Corinthians 5:16–21
Every generous act of giving, with every perfect gift, is from above, coming down from the Father of lights, with whom there is no variation or shadow due to change.
James 1:17 (NRSV)

Our town was buried by a record snowfall. Walking outside, I noticed the tracks of animals of many different kinds, even animals I had never seen in my neighbourhood before.

I was reminded of a time when the heaviness of life, like that snowfall, had hit me with full force. Alone in a hospital waiting room, I learned that my mother's exploratory surgery had revealed terminal cancer. As the surgeon left me, a friend from church came around the corner and said, 'Just thought I would see if you are all right.' My stunned silence turned to sobbing as I collapsed into her arms.

My friend's presence just then was just the gift I needed. But how many times had I taken such a simple kindness for granted? Are acts of love, like the silent tracks of creatures on my snowy walk, treasured only when the bleakness of life make them obvious?

Thinking about my day so far reminds me that evidence of God's love is all around me: a kiss on the cheek from my husband, an 'I love you, Mum' note from my son, the laughter of neighbours chatting in the garden. Even though the snow is melting, I can choose to treasure the 'love tracks' in my life today and every day.

Prayer: *God of all comfort, remind us each day to notice the tracks of love and care you have left in our lives. May we never take for granted the special people you place on our path. Amen*

Thought for the day: Today, I will leave love tracks in the lives of those near me.

Shannon Hale (Missouri, US)

Follow Me

Read 1 Corinthians 10:31—11:1
Be imitators of me, as I am of Christ.
1 Corinthians 11:1 (NIV)

'Follow me,' I instructed my son-in-law. We were driving in separate cars to a restaurant in a part of town he did not know. As I started down the road, I felt I had to drive slowly. As we made the necessary turns, I was careful to signal well in advance. I kept a close eye on him in my mirror to confirm that he was following me and did not get lost. In the end, we all arrived at the restaurant for an enjoyable lunch together.

That day, it occurred to me that believers are charged with the task of being an example for others to follow, leading them to Christ. As we find ourselves at work or at school or in our leisure time, our actions are being viewed and evaluated by others. As we direct our lives toward heaven, we can bring others with us by living a life that models the life of Jesus Christ.

Prayer: *Dear Lord, remind us that the actions of our lives show others the way to our destination. May our actions always direct them to Christ and his eternal glory in heaven. Amen*

Thought for the day: If someone's going to follow me, I want to lead that person to Christ.

Mary Ziober (Louisiana, US)

What is Right

Read 2 Kings 18:1–16

Hezekiah prayed, 'Remember, Lord, how I have walked before you faithfully and with wholehearted devotion and have done what is good in your eyes.'

2 Kings 20:3 (NIV)

In the Old Testament, people's lives are repeatedly classified in one of two ways, as a sort of scriptural eulogy: he did evil in the eyes of the Lord or he did what was right in the eyes of the Lord.

I rarely consider my life in such simple terms. Media messages entice me to dwell on how nice I look as I age, the type of decor in my home and what I do for a living. It is easy to forget that—in the light of eternity—obedience to God is much more important than such trivialities.

It can be tempting to ignore God's standard of selfless love, but all those life summaries in the Old Testament remind me that my choices need to be anchored to something bigger than I and bigger than my shifting emotions. My choices should revolve around God and what pleases him. When God reflects on the sum of my life—who I was and what I did—I want to hear, 'She did what is good in the eyes of the Lord.'

Prayer: *Help us, O God, to love you with all our hearts and with all our souls and with all our strength, and to love our neighbours as ourselves. Amen*

Thought for the day: Today I can choose to do what is right in the eyes of the Lord.

Holly Dickson-Ramos (Ontario, Canada)

PRAYER FOCUS: SOMEONE FACING A SERIOUS CHOICE

31

Praising God

Read Psalm 63

Let us continually offer a sacrifice of praise to God, that is, the fruit of lips that confess his name.
Hebrews 13:15 (NRSV)

Recently, for two consecutive days, the set reading in my devotions was Psalm 63. So I asked the Lord, 'What are you trying to tell me?'

Verse 7 of the psalm says, 'I sing in the shadow of your wings' (NIV). Sometimes shadows are a welcome thing, such as when we want relief from a too-bright sun, and it is easy to sing praises to the Lord at a time like that.

At other times the shadows are those of obstacles in our path, such as grief, sickness or sorrow. It is much harder to praise God in times like this when everything seems hard or is going wrong. However, then it struck me that the very presence of these shadows is proof of the sunlight beyond. You cannot have a shadow unless there is a light to cast it.

If we were not aware that God is in control beyond our current difficulties and that he knows all things, it would be even harder to sing.

Prayer: *We thank you, Lord, that we can offer you a sacrifice of praise in the shadowed times as well as a hymn of praise in the sunnier days.*

Thought for the day: I can praise God no matter what my circumstances.

Hilary Hartley (Sussex, England)

Midday Peace

Read Psalm 23:1–3
After [Jesus] had dismissed the crowds, he went up the mountain by himself to pray. When evening came, he was there alone.
Matthew 14:23 (NRSV)

When I changed jobs a few years ago, I started going to a local park in my lunch hour. Even in the winter months, I try to walk once around the park so that I can breathe in the fresh air and be in God's presence. Time away from office noise, stress and artificial light allows me to focus my mind so that I can tackle the afternoon with a renewed sense of energy.

Jesus took time for himself as well. Even though he was surrounded by so many people and under a huge amount of stress, he took time alone to speak to his Father. He used the time—surrounded by nature and away from his disciples and the crowds—to cry out, to be vulnerable and to find the strength to carry on. If Jesus can take a moment for prayer and meditation, why can't we?

Psalm 23 tells us that God leads us to quiet pastures and still waters to refresh our souls. My daily walks have helped me to see what God has provided for me in the trees, water, wind and wildlife. My lunchtime walks help me to maintain a peaceful attitude and renew my faith.

Prayer: *Dear Lord, thank you for giving us time to enjoy the natural world and to find peace with you. Amen*

Thought for the day: Taking time away brings us closer to God.

Sue Fairchild (Pennsylvania, US)

A Simple Question

Read 2 Kings 22:11—23:3

Thou shalt not take the name of the Lord thy God in vain.
Exodus 20:7 (KJV)

'Ginger, do you love God?' my friend Sherry asked.

'Well, yes! You know I do.' I was shocked by this question. Sherry talked with me every day on our breaks, and we discussed our faith and life in general. We had come to know a lot about each other, or at least I thought we did—until I heard this question. We had talked about the changes we had been through and how God had delivered each of us.

'Then why do you constantly take God's name in vain?' Just like that, she had let the wind out of my sails. I accepted the loving admonishment and made a change that very day. I wasn't brought up to disrespect God in any way, big or small.

King Josiah also knew he needed to make a change. When a book of the law was found, he had it interpreted by the prophetess Huldah. The interpretation let him and the people know that they had abandoned God and that God was angry.

Just like Josiah, I began a new relationship with God. I thanked Sherry that day for pointing out something that I had been too careless or blind to see. I'll never forget how much love she showed for me and for God with one simple question.

Prayer: *Dear God, you know our hearts and that our desire is to be close to you. Correct us when we wander from your path. Amen*

Thought for the day: How do my words express my love for God?

Ginger Robinson (Texas, US)

Secret Things

Read Deuteronomy 29:2-6, 29
The secret things belong to the Lord our God, but the revealed things belong to us and to our children for ever, to observe all the words of this law.
Deuteronomy 29:29 (NRSV)

When I went away to college, I discovered many new ideas. As a very earnest young Christian, I struggled to reconcile the new things I was learning—especially in philosophy and religious studies—with the simple doctrines I had been taught in church. When I questioned my minister about my struggles, his advice was that I should just avoid thinking about such things.

My grandmother lived with us, and one day when I was at home during a holiday, her pastor came to visit. He asked how college was going. I said, 'Fine.' But he must have sensed something in my voice, because he dug deeper and engaged me in real conversation about my questions and struggles. Finally, he quoted to me the words of Deuteronomy 29:29.

The words of this verse spoke to me deeply and suggested to me that it is OK not to know everything. Some things are 'secret things' and they will always remain a mystery. It is good to question, to explore new ideas, to expand our minds as far as we can. But some questions will never be settled with a final answer. No matter how clever we are or how educated we become, we will reach a point where intellect can take us no further. At that point, we can rely on faith, hope and love to carry us the rest of the way.

Prayer: *Dear God, grant us wisdom as we explore the mysteries of your universe, and help us to be faithful in following you. Amen*

Thought for the day: God's majesty is beyond our understanding.

David Fillingim (North Carolina, US)

Spring Scents

Read Psalm 19:7–11

The Sovereign Lord declares, 'I will give you a new heart and put a new spirit in you; I will remove from you your heart of stone and give you a heart of flesh.'
Ezekiel 36:26 (NIV)

Our garden was created in part to make the most of the amazing scents of spring. It includes violets, lavender, freesias and lilac. This spring, I could see the beauty of these lovely plants and hear the bees busily at work, but I couldn't enjoy the heady scents of the plants. As a lingering effect of a particularly difficult bout of bronchitis my sense of smell was affected. I felt cut off from fully enjoying this season I love.

The situation made me think about my spiritual life. At times I feel totally 'in tune' with God, and life seems fulfilling and complete. But at other times I feel more distant from God—as though I am going through the motions rather than being fully alive to him. That's when life seems frustrating or dissatisfying. It's not that God has moved away from me; it's that I've allowed other things to get in the way of my relationship with him.

When any of us experiences such a time and then turns back to God, we don't need to worry about being given the cold shoulder. Instead, he is there, with open arms, to welcome us back.

Prayer: *Loving Father, help us to become ever more responsive to you. May our lives be filled with you—your love, your Spirit and your goodness. Amen*

Thought for the day: Am I filling my life with God—or something else?

Meg Mangan (New South Wales, Australia)

Depending on Each Other

Read Ephesians 4:11–16

The boy's father exclaimed, 'I do believe; help me overcome my unbelief!'
Mark 9:24 (NIV)

I used to think that faith has a static quality, that a person possesses either all or none of it. But through the years I have learned that faith can waver. When our faith is strong it is very important to show our faith through our actions and in our words. Because of our faith, others can claim the courage to believe when belief seems impossible. They can be made strong again because they can, in their doubt, trust in our faith.

When our faith is weak, we can rely on the faith of those around us. In times of struggle and transition, I always know that my friends are praying for me. Despite their own afflictions, they have the faith to rally round me. In their devotion and steadfastness, I see God working through them.

It is OK to cling to the faith of others. God's church was designed to be a community of interdependent believers. Abiding faith will draw the seekers and sustain the doubters. When our faith is strong, we can reach out in Christian concern for those around us and, even amidst a world of doubt, we can reassure others that faith abides.

Prayer: *Dear God, remind us to share our living and active faith with others and to rely on others when our faith wavers. Amen*

Thought for the day: Believers are an interdependent community.

Suzanne Dyer (California, US)

The Thorn Bush

Read 1 Peter 2:21–24
We are healed by the punishment he suffered.
Isaiah 53:5 (GNB)

After a blustery, wet winter's night it seemed that all the litter in the park was pinned to a solitary thorn bush. The bush appeared to have an item on every spike, like an over-dressed Christmas tree: crisp packets, chocolate and biscuit wrappers, shredded tissues, plastic cups and a whole assortment of paper in a rainbow of soggy colours. My first reaction was to be appalled at the ugliness of the burdened branches. Then I noticed the grass all around me—lush green. It was fresh, swept clean by the ferocious winds.

As I continued my walk, my mind made a swift connection between the bush and the words of Peter—'by his wounds you have been healed'—and I thought of the cross.

Jesus, like the thorn bush, had faced the cruel onslaught of evil, to carry all the rubbish of human life, and by his courageous, self-giving sacrifice has cleaned up the world. I turned back to look again at the bush, and my heart said, 'The Saviour! My Lord and my God!'

Prayer: *Lord Jesus Christ, you took on yourself the sin of the whole world—and mine— and made it clean. Thank you. Amen*

Thought for the day: A life of love is like the littered thorn bush in the park.

Colin D. Harbach (Cumbria, England)

The Shepherd's Voice

Read John 10:22–30

A cloud appeared and covered them, and a voice came from the cloud:
'This is my Son, whom I love. Listen to him!'
Mark 9:7 (NIV)

My husband and I took a trip to the shopping centre one day with our eight-month-old son. While my husband entertained our son, I enjoyed some 'me time', window shopping alone. But after a while I heard a loud, happy squeal piercing through the crowd. Immediately able to identify the screamer, I whipped my head around and spotted my husband and son a great distance away. Our son was waving happily and blowing me kisses. Even among the thousands of other sounds filling the crowded shops that day, I distinguished the sound of my son's voice.

This experience reminds me of my relationship with Christ. Through an intimate relationship with Christ, I am learning to distinguish his voice, even amidst the clamour of the world. John 10:27–28 says, 'My sheep listen to my voice; I know them, and they follow me. I give them eternal life, and they shall never perish; no one will snatch them out of my hand.'

My son is a part of me, and I am a part of him. Sheep know their shepherd's voice because of the time and care a shepherd invests in them. Our Shepherd is a part of us and we are part of him.

Prayer: *Dear Lord, help us decipher your voice over the sounds of the world. Amen*

Thought for the day: Today I will listen for my Shepherd's voice over the clamour of this world.

Michelle S. Lazurek (Pennsylvania, US)

A Milkshake?

Read 1 Thessalonians 5:12–24
Encourage the disheartened.
1 Thessalonians 5:14 (NIV)

Living as a missionary, I meet some great people. One of them, Kathy, once drove me almost an hour to get to an office so that we could sort out an issue with my visa. When we finally got there, they told us they would not be able to help us; we would need to come back later. I felt like a fool for wasting Kathy's time and petrol. But do you know what she said to me? 'Would you like a milkshake?'

Sometimes it's the small things that surprise me most. In that moment, Kathy's offer certainly surprised me. So she bought us milkshakes and took that opportunity to tell me about how she started mission work. It was like hearing a modern story from the book of Acts. Her husband died and she was left alone, so she sold her house to join a missionary team. She gave up everything she had to help people in need. She acted in faith and is now for me a living picture of being like Christ. At the age of 65 she exhibits joy and encouragement—and it's all because of Christ.

Prayer: *Dear Lord, you have encouraged us in many ways. Help us to be encouraging to others. Amen*

Thought for the day: Today I will encourage someone in their faith.

Gabriel Brennan (KwaZulu-Natal, South Africa)

Are You Weary?

Read Matthew 11:28–30
Whoever dwells in the shelter of the Most High will rest in the shadow of the Almighty.
Psalm 91:1 (NIV)

In my therapeutic massage practice, I see many women who are tired, worn out, sick, hurting and unable to sleep. They tell me they have no time for themselves. They always have things to do and to achieve—meetings, family obligations, work, housework. The list is endless. We put a lot of stress on our bodies when we don't allow ourselves time to rest and recover, and we tend to ignore the warning signs when we have pushed ourselves too far.

The Bible tells us that we are to work, but it also tells us to rest. We often find it difficult to achieve a balance between the two. God commands us to rest. Listening to our bodies' cries to slow down isn't easy. However, if we hand over all our cares and worries to God each day and put our focus on him and not on the world around us, we will discover over time that rest becomes easier.

Prayer: *Dear God, we give you our cares and worries today. Please be with us as we go about our daily lives and help us to rest. Amen*

Thought for the day: When we go to God with our daily struggles, we find rest.

Susan Tedrow (Indiana, US)

41

Sin that Dams

Read 1 John 1:5—2:2
If we confess our sins, he who is faithful and just will forgive us our sins and cleanse us from all unrighteousness.
1 John 1:9 (NRSV)

After the storm had passed, I strolled down to the creek. The two-year drought we had experienced was finally over, and I was delighted to see the waterway filling. To the left, the current carried the water along its natural course; to the right, however, a pool of stagnant water rested against some debris.

The storm had washed leaves, sticks, grass and rubbish into the creek bed, and it was caught on a log. This created a dam that prevented the water from flowing freely. If allowed to stay, the pooled water would attract mosquitoes, create an odour and become contaminated. It needed to be cleaned out.

Sin is like that debris. We may not notice many problems from a few minor infractions. But left alone to collect and pile, these sins will clog the path to life and freedom. Habitual sin—such as pride, gluttony, lying and idolatry—creates a barrier and blocks our relationship with God and others. The result of the obstruction, a stagnant spiritual life, attracts further sin and spills over into other areas of our lives. The obstruction that sin creates in our lives needs to be cleaned out. Thankfully, we have a remedy—repentance (see Acts 3:19).

Prayer: *Dear heavenly Father, reveal our sins to us. Help us repent so that we may have a closer relationship with you and live life more abundantly. Amen*

Thought for the day: Abundant life is available to all who seek it.

Barb Winters (Illinois, US)

Never Give Up

Read Philippians 3:7–16

I want to know Christ and the power of his resurrection and the sharing of his sufferings by becoming like him in his death, if somehow I may attain the resurrection from the dead.

Philippians 3:10–11 (NRSV)

I was enjoying my lunch in the park when I saw a couple training their son to kick a ball between two cones. At first the child could not kick the ball between the cones many times in a row, but he never gave up until finally he could do so consistently.

Similarly, chapter 3 of Paul's letter to the Philippians reveals a heart that never gives up. From Paul's relationship with Jesus came the fruit of his fervour. And because of this, Paul was able to guide others to faith in God.

If our goal is merely serving the Lord, we may burn out soon. But if our goal is like Paul's, that is to know Christ, we will find that he is our true source of strength—enabling us to make him known to others.

I never want to give up in my efforts to serve Christ joyfully, who is the source of my strength.

Prayer: *Dear God, we want to know you more fully. In your strength may we never give up but serve you joyfully. Amen*

Thought for the day: To know Christ is to serve joyfully each day.

Mary Ng (Singapore)

In the Palm of God's Hand

Read Isaiah 43:1–7

I have inscribed you on the palms of my hands.
Isaiah 49:16 (NRSV)

Like her name, Ruby is a jewel. No longer able to come to church, she had found it hard to give up her bungalow and go into care, and she is now in her nineties and bedridden.

A few of us gathered around her bedside to share Holy Communion with her, but we found her anxious and confused. We might get into trouble. We must not sing. Gently, our minister led us all in the wonderful service as we remembered the death of our Saviour for us.

Ruby's fears were dispelled as she received the bread and wine that had been so familiar to her through the years. Then something wonderful happened: she began to sing. Her voice was weak, but her words were clear.

'I am in the palm of his hand.' Cuddled up in her pillows, Ruby had her hand cupped near to her face as though she was holding a precious treasure. Undoubtedly this was how she pictured herself: eternally safe and secure, loved and treasured in the palm of God's hand.

We know that Ruby's Saviour, and ours too, has promised to give us songs in the night, and that we are all safe in the palm of his hand.

Prayer: *Dear Lord, help us, whatever happens, to know that we are safe and secure with you. Amen*

Thought for the day: I will be thankful for God's love today.

Pauline Lewis (South Wales)

Endurance

Read Hebrews 12:1–6

Let us run with perseverance the race that is set before us, looking to Jesus.
Hebrews 12:1–2 (NRSV)

At school, our cross-country team often practised running barefoot on the beach. Being inexperienced, we resented our coach for making us train under those conditions. It was miserable and almost impossible to run with any speed. Our time records were downright discouraging. We did, however, develop amazing strength and endurance. Even so, we whined and complained the entire time—until our first race, in which we finished way ahead of the other teams.

The constant fighting and struggling, barefoot, through the soft, shifting sand dunes had forced us to become conscious of every step, to steady our footing, to toughen up and to push on through the pain and resistance. When the resistance was finally removed, the race was easy and we were victorious.

Sometimes, we become discouraged when God allows resistance to come into our lives. We whine and complain, not realising that God is not allowing those circumstances in order to tear us down, but instead to build us up. Whenever we are frustrated, we can become stronger if we trust in God's wisdom, keep pressing forward and run the race with perseverance.

Prayer: *Dear Lord, thank you for your wisdom and faithfulness that strengthens us when we encounter resistance in our lives. Amen*

Thought for the day: As we persevere to overcome obstacles in our lives, God gives us strength.

Kathy Thomas (Florida, US)

PRAYER FOCUS: THAT WE WILL NOT BE DISCOURAGED   45

House Cleaning

Read Psalm 119:25–29
[Jesus] said to them, 'Come away to a deserted place all by yourselves and rest a while.'
Mark 6:31 (NRSV)

Resting in my chair after a family gathering, I noticed cobwebs between the corner and a beam in the ceiling. I thought I had cleaned my house well. How did I miss those? I realised that I had not taken the time to look up. It was only when I sat down to rest that I looked up and caught sight of a neglected spot in my home.

In a spiritual sense, when our minds and hearts are consumed with busyness, we miss the places in our lives that need cleaning. With our heads down, trying to organise the clutter of our lives, we think we're focused on what's important, and so we forget to make time for spiritual rest. Raising our eyes upward in prayer to give God thanks and praise, we open a line of communication with the One who can provide rest to our souls. During intimate times with God in prayer and Bible reading, he can show us the places in our lives that need attention—a bad habit, a wrong attitude or an unwillingness to forgive.

By spending time today in spiritual rest, we allow God to reveal the unattended places in our hearts. Then we can examine the way we're living and let him help us to brush away the cobwebs that have appeared from neglect of our spiritual house.

Prayer: *Dear Lord, as we rest in you, show us the places in our hearts that we have neglected. Give us courage to clean as you lead. Amen*

Thought for the day: Resting with God gives us a new perspective.

Beth Fortune (South Carolina, US)

Simple Wonders

Read Luke 12:22–31

'Don't be afraid. You are worth more than many sparrows.'
Matthew 10:31 (CEB)

One sunny afternoon, I was dwelling on my many problems. Some weeks before, I had applied for several jobs, but with no results. With no more openings available—and constantly reminded that all my friends had good careers—I was feeling depressed and stuck. Then I looked around and noticed the works of God's hand right in front of me. I looked up to see beauty: Mount Sindoro, Mount Sumbing and even Dieng Plateau, so strong and majestic. The golden light of sunset warmed my skin. I heard birds singing, and the cool afternoon breeze made me realise that in spite of my burdens, God had not neglected me. He was delighting me with little surprises, the recognition of simple wonders I see every day but rarely notice. And when I saw all God's creation in front of me, I remembered that Jesus said, 'You are worth so much more than birds!' (Luke 12:24).

God lovingly cares for all creation—birds, flowers, mountains and especially us. Even though our problems continue, so also does the knowledge that the hand that takes care of creation is the same hand that takes care of us. I feel very blessed. Problems may come and go, but through it all the providence of God sustains us.

Prayer: *Dear God, thank you for your love that helps us face our problems without worry and fear. Amen*

Thought for the day: God's love is revealed in the wonders of nature.

Yohana Defrita Rufikasari (Central Java, Indonesia)

Remember

Read Hebrews 11:1–39

I will call to mind the deeds of the Lord; I will remember your wonders of old.

Psalm 77:11 (NRSV)

When I was a child, my family lived with my grandparents and my uncle. My uncle loved to tell family stories. Through his stories I learned that I had my grandfather's nose, that my great-aunt also loved to write, and that my talent for cooking came from my mother's older sister. I learned also about the big farm where they all lived. Because of my uncle's storytelling I began to know who I was and where I came from.

The Bible is like my uncle's stories. I need to know about my ancestors in the faith, about God's mighty acts, and about the love that he has for me. Because I am part of the family of God, I need to know who I am and what God's dreams are for me. I can discover this through the Bible and its stories of the family of God.

I need to spend time with my Bible every day, learning and remembering the stories so that I can live as part of God's family in the world.

Prayer: *Loving Father, thank you for the stories you have given us. Please help us to remember who we are through your stories and to share them with others. Amen*

Thought for the day: Remembering our faith stories leads us closer to God.

Eugenie Daniels (Massachusetts, US)

Life in the Blood

Read Ezekiel 36:25–27

In Christ Jesus you who once were far away have been brought near by the blood of Christ.
Ephesians 2:13 (NIV)

A few years ago I worked as a nurse in a cardiology lab. Frequently I participated in certain heart procedures for patients who were close to death because of heart disease. Nothing thrilled me more than to see the miracle of a partially dead heart come back to life when the balloon was inflated to open up a blocked artery.

This sudden rush of blood from the newly opened artery then enters and revives the dead heart muscle with fresh oxygen. That dead muscle, which has been more like a stone than a living organ, becomes flesh and is able to pump blood more effectively to the rest of the patient's body. In fact, many of those patients would die quickly if their arteries were not reopened.

Seeing lives revived by the introduction of new blood brought to my mind the verse from Leviticus 17:11, 'The life of a creature is in the blood… it is the blood that makes atonement for one's life.' Also when I read in Ezekiel how God will remove our 'heart of stone' and give us a 'heart of flesh', I think about my own heart having been dead before I accepted Jesus.

I see now how God's Spirit infused my own heart of stone with the blood of Jesus, bringing me to everlasting life. My heart is now alive and I have new life, both here on earth and for all eternity with Christ.

Prayer: *Dear Jesus, thank you for reviving our hearts by your Holy Spirit. Amen*

Thought for the day: The power of eternal life comes from the blood of Jesus.

Deanne Ruedemann (Texas, US)

A Father's Pride

Read Mark 1:9–13

The Lord takes delight in his people.
Psalm 149:4 (NIV)

Even when my dad struggled with alcohol addiction, he made it clear to me that he loved me and was proud of me. Sadly, some people never hear encouraging words from their fathers. They feel a huge void in their lives because the one man in the world whom they want to please the most isn't there for them.

After Jesus had been baptised and when he emerged from the water, he heard a voice from heaven saying, 'You are my Son, whom I love; with you I am well pleased' (Mark 1:11). Then the Spirit sent him into the wilderness. He didn't pack anything; he didn't say goodbye to anyone. All he took with him was his Father's approval and pride. That was all Jesus needed to endure 40 days of temptation from Satan.

I'm grateful that over time my father achieved sobriety, and we've had the opportunity to repair the brokenness that kept us apart. But regardless of our relationships with our earthly fathers, we have a heavenly Father who can fill all the holes in our lives. This heavenly Father knows us, loves us and is well pleased with us—simply because we are his beloved.

Prayer: *Heavenly Father, thank you for always loving us. Help us to see ourselves through your eyes. In Jesus' name we pray. Amen*

Thought for the day: God's love is more important than any earthly approval.

Justin Farrell (Washington, US)

Adjusting to Change

Read Isaiah 42:5–10

I press on toward the goal for the prize of the heavenly call of God in Christ Jesus.
Philippians 3:14 (NRSV)

As our music group, Joyful Noise, began practising a new song, I could not seem to get the correct rhythm. With a degree in music education, I rarely have problems reading music. Why now? Reading the words, I realised that the new song was actually an old one. In the new version, however, the words were set to a syncopated rhythm rather than the familiar, simple 4/4 beat I had played for years. Even though I could read the music, I kept slipping back into the familiar beat.

This experience reminded me how difficult change can be. Our church is currently experiencing change as our much-loved pastor of eight years assumes responsibility for a new congregation and we prepare to welcome a new pastor. Although we want to hold on to what we know and love, we need to open our hearts to what God has in store for us. In his final sermon to our congregation, our pastor admonished us to press on. We honour him and our Lord as we press on under new leadership.

The only constant any of us has is the promise that 'Jesus Christ is the same yesterday and today and for ever' (Hebrews 13:8, NIV). Circumstances may change, but Christ's message remains the same.

Prayer: *Dear God, help us to release the past and to go forth in Jesus' name. Amen*

Thought for the day: God will lead us through changing seasons.

Pat Watson (Texas, US)

A Big God

Read Psalm 27:1–6

If God is for us, who can be against us?
Romans 8:31 (NIV)

I work as a tutor. Before she moved up to the next class, one of my youngest students said to me, 'This would've been hard, but because you're here with me, I don't have to worry.'

Her simple words reminded me of my journey with God. Sometimes I feel fear in the midst of life's severe problems. I worry and often cannot sleep. The fear makes me forget that an almighty God is always beside me. In fact, he is never far away from any of us.

I wonder if I am as eager to trust in God as fully as my young student trusts in me. If I can trust him that much, every time I face a problem I can say, 'If God is for [me], who can be against [me]?' And instead of saying, 'God, I have a big problem', I can say, 'Hey, problem, I have a big God!'

Prayer: *Almighty God, help us not to worry and to trust that you are always near and will never leave us. As Jesus taught us, we pray, 'Our Father in heaven, hallowed be your name, your kingdom come, your will be done, on earth as it is in heaven. Give us today our daily bread. And forgive us our debts, as we also have forgiven our debtors. And lead us not into temptation, but deliver us from the evil one.'* Amen*

Thought for the day: Because God is near, I need not fear.

Linawati Santoso (East Java, Indonesia)

PRAYER FOCUS: SCHOOL PUPILS
* Matthew 6:9–13 (NIV)

A Deeper Longing

Read Exodus 33:12–23

Without faith it is impossible to please God, because anyone who comes to him must believe that he exists and that he rewards those who earnestly seek him.
Hebrews 11:6 (NIV)

Seeking God is the first step of faith for those who want to know, understand and follow God, who desires fellowship with us. I learned this lesson from my friend Brenda, whose life is a witness to me. Her everyday behaviour is a message to me from the Holy Spirit.

When I was struggling to see God, Brenda had the spiritual insight I was missing. I realised that she practises noticing and acknowledging God's presence minute-by-minute every day. I have learned that the power of the Holy Spirit is more available to us when we practise consciously living in God's presence. I want to live that way every day.

Our efforts glorify God when we praise and thank him aloud and when we encourage and accept other people. Graciousness, joy and peace are God's gifts to us so that we can be grateful servants, witnessing for him.

Prayer: *Dear God, thank you for wanting a living conversation with us. Make us more aware of your presence each moment of the day. In Jesus' name, we pray. Amen*

Thought for the day: Living in God's presence gives peace to our souls.

Ruth Ann Dalley (California, US)

The True Treasure

Read Ecclesiastes 2:1–11

'Do not store up for yourselves treasures on earth, where moths and vermin destroy, and where thieves break in and steal. But store up for yourselves treasures in heaven… For where your treasure is, there your heart will be also.'
Matthew 6:19–21 (NIV)

My mother has dementia, and she is no longer able to live alone. Last year she went to live in a nursing home, and now I'm emptying her house to sell it. For 50 years she accumulated many treasured possessions—furniture, china, clothes, shoes, letters, books and photos to name a few—seemingly never throwing anything away. Today, most of these things have little or no monetary value. In a few days her possessions will be sold, given away or thrown out.

While doing this difficult task, I've never so clearly understood the words in Ecclesiastes: 'Everything was meaningless, a chasing after the wind' (Ecclesiastes 2:11). It occurred to me that accumulating possessions is not of any value once our earthly lives are over.

Now it is time for me to refocus my priorities and my efforts, not on the material things of this world but on the kingdom of God, on justice and on my relationship with Jesus and with others. That is the real treasure Matthew 6 speaks about. This treasure will never lose its value and will never be thrown away. This treasure will always be with us, in eternity.

Prayer: *Dear Lord Jesus, help us to discern the important things in life—our relationship with you and with others. Amen*

Thought for the day: The best things in life come from God.

Daniel Sebbah (Provence-Alpes-Côte d'Azur, France)

Baptised

Read 1 Peter 3:18–22
The one who believes and is baptised will be saved.
Mark 16:16 (NRSV)

Years ago, my husband and I attended a small church in California, where we started our family. Once in a sermon the pastor told us that his mother had framed her children's baptismal certificates and hung them above their beds. They could rest assured as children of God.

Remembering this story, I recently decided to find our baptismal certificates, frame them and hang them above our bed. As I did, my mind travelled back through the years of my life that have been enriched by the assurance of God's love. Our heavenly Father gave his only son, Jesus Christ, to suffer and die for us, to save us from all our sins when we repent of our disobedience and turn to the love of God.

To me, the most important part of my life is the fact that I was baptised. I am thankful that through baptism, God bestows on us the gift of the Holy Spirit to be our companion, guide and comfort.

Prayer: *Thank you, God, for the gift of baptism and for salvation through Jesus Christ our Lord. Amen*

Thought for the day: What is my visual reminder of God's love?

Helen Bliss (Washington, US)

Stop, Look, Listen

Read Psalm 46:1-11

The Lord came and stood there, calling as at the other times, 'Samuel! Samuel!' Then Samuel said, 'Speak, for your servant is listening.'
1 Samuel 3:10 (NIV)

My life can be hectic and hurried: rushing out to work, caring for children and other loved ones, preparing meals, dealing with unexpected interruptions and emergencies. Some days, I don't slow down until I tumble into bed.

Early in the year our minister offered us a challenge: 'Slow down. Let God get your attention. Look around. Listen. Take five minutes each day to notice life.'

I accepted the challenge, and the results have been surprising. I stopped to watch the purples and pinks of a sunset become more vivid with each passing minute. I noticed movement behind my house and saw deer, romping like children. I lit a fire on a cold night and felt its warmth surround me. I listened as a friend talked about the challenges she faced. Her comments helped me to deal with situations in my own life.

By slowing down for a few moments to be open to God and the life around me, I saw that each day is full of blessings. The challenge is to take time to notice.

Prayer: *Dear God, thank you for the many blessings that come to us each day. Help us to slow down and to appreciate all that you give us. Amen*

Thought for the day: Today I will slow down and be thankful for life's blessings.

Valerie Battle Kienzle (Missouri, US)

A Matter of Appearances

Read Titus 3:3–8

'A good tree cannot bear bad fruit, and a bad tree cannot bear good fruit... Thus, by their fruit you will recognise them.'
Matthew 7:18, 20 (NIV)

I remember once when I was a young teenager, my mother asked me to go to a local shop and get a few things for her. Then she looked at my scruffy clothes and said, 'Change your clothes and tidy yourself up first. What would people think of me if they saw you looking like that?' Mother believed that the way I appeared in public was a reflection on her.

Although early Christians had to be careful not to talk openly about their faith for fear of persecution, they did reflect their faith in their behaviour and attitudes. By their example, many others were brought to Christ. Things haven't changed much in this regard. Those we meet along the way notice our habits and attitudes. They draw conclusions about our beliefs based on our outward demeanour and behaviour. If our words claim Christianity yet our behaviour testifies otherwise, people will conclude that our actions reflect the truth about us.

Today I am old enough to be retired, but I still remember that my behaviour and way of living cast a reflection on those whom I love and those who love me. I can say with words that I am a Christian, but actions that reflect true Christian love speak louder than anything.

Prayer: *Dear God, let us praise you not only with the words of our mouths but also with our actions. Amen*

Thought for the day: My actions and words can show God's love to others.

Gale A. Richards (Iowa, US)

PRAYER FOCUS: TEENAGERS

Broken Connections

Read Romans 12:9–21

Rejoice in hope, be patient in suffering, persevere in prayer.
Romans 12:12 (NRSV)

I turned on the tap, but no water came out. I ran to check the pump in the shed. It was still working, but a pipe had broken. Gushing bursts of water had covered the shed floor and water was flowing away, wasting a valuable resource. By disconnecting the power I was finally able to turn off the water supply to the large storage tank that was draining water into the now muddy back garden.

Being securely connected is important in our relationship with God. To maintain healthy spiritual lives, we need to be connected through Christ in prayer and then maintained and nurtured by the word and the Holy Spirit. If one link in this connection is broken, the precious flow of God in our lives and our abilities to care, to love and to be strong in faith may be drained away by the eroding circumstances of daily life. In times like these our connection to God can sustain us.

Prayer: *Dear Lord, help us to be disciplined in our time with you so that we remain securely connected to you in prayer, word and spirit. Amen*

Thought for the day: How can I nurture my relationship with God?

Faye Roots (Queensland, Australia)

Honour Your Father

Read Hebrews 12:7–11
We have all had human fathers who disciplined us and we respected them for it. How much more should we submit to the Father of spirits and live!
Hebrews 12:9 (NIV)

My father was known for his 'I'll-give-you-the shirt-off-my-back' generosity. But when I asked him for some money to buy a toy from a classmate, I was surprised when he responded quietly and thoughtfully, 'No.' He explained that the toy was a want, not a need.

The next day when my father was out, I opened his desk drawer, stole some money and bought the toy. A few days later, when he discovered that the money was missing, he knew immediately that I was the thief. He told me I had no reason to steal from him. I could depend on his promise to give me everything I needed. He expressed a deep disappointment in me, yet ended his stern reprimand by saying, 'But I still love you.'

When I reflect on how my father handled my disobedience, it became clear to me that he exemplified the kind of love that God, my heavenly Father, has for me even when I fall short.

God said, 'Honour your father' (Exodus 20:12). Today and every day I honour my father for his loving discipline, and I give thanks for the unconditional love that God shows to us.

Prayer: *Dear God, thank you for the example of loving earthly parents and for your unconditional love for all of your children. Amen*

Thought for the day: Even in my disobedience, God loves me.

Suzanne S. Austin-Hill (Florida, US)

With All Your Heart

Read Luke 5:1-11
The Lord declares, 'You will seek me and find me when you seek me with all your heart.'
Jeremiah 29:13 (NIV)

For years I taught history. When the end of the term approached, I would offer students the opportunity to improve their results by doing an additional assignment. Some eagerly complied and earned better results. Others would shrug with a 'Thanks, but no thanks' attitude, content with a lower mark.

Half-hearted efforts achieve half-hearted results. The consequences of a lower history mark may be minor, but when responding to God the outcome is far more important. Through Jeremiah the Lord promises, 'You will seek me and find me when you seek me with all your heart.' I believe God is warning us that this tendency to put forth less than our full effort may spill over into our spiritual lives.

Luke tells us about Jesus' early encounter with Simon, James and John on the lake shore. Though they had fished all night unsuccessfully, Jesus instructed them to row out and drop their nets again. When they obeyed, not only did they have a net-breaking catch of fish, but the three men left everything and followed Christ. That is living wholeheartedly! To be truly used and blessed by God, we must we willing to do the same.

Prayer: *Guide of humanity, help us to follow you boldly. Amen*

Thought for the day: Am I living wholeheartedly for Christ?

Lisa Stackpole (Wisconsin, US)

Path Markers

Read Psalm 32:6–10
I will instruct you and teach you in the way you should go.
Psalm 32:8 (NIV)

I am a trailblazer, pathfinder and guide. In the area where I work, we have ways to guide hikers along the path. Wherever a junction of paths occurs, a sign and a coloured footprint indicate the new route. Once hikers are on the right path, rocks painted with white dots have been placed roughly 50 paces apart to indicate the way to go. When the path is slightly overgrown, some hikers begin to feel a bit anxious, wondering if they are still on the right path. At such times, they are relieved to spot a white mark on a rock so they can confidently proceed on their way.

Walking with God through our daily lives is similar to hiking a well-marked trail. God has promised to guide us and show the way at each important new junction. When no guidance seems to come, we may begin to feel anxious, wondering if we are still walking in the 'Way of God'. That is when God's 'white dots' are so encouraging. Each 'dot' or sign could be described as a nod from him, indicating that we are still on the right path and that he is pleased with our progress. 'Just keep following the path you are on,' God seems to be saying. 'I will show you when to turn off next.' These signs may appear in the form of scripture, words from a friend or part of a sermon. Even circumstances can play a part in confirming God's signs.

Prayer: *Dear Lord, open our eyes that we may see your guidance on our path and lead others to a better understanding of you. Amen*

Thought for the day: God is our best possible guide through life.

Gerald McCann (Western Cape, South Africa)

PRAYER FOCUS: SOMEONE STRUGGLING WITH A DECISION   61

Thinking Backwards

Read 2 Corinthians 4:18—5:1

We fix our eyes not on what is seen, but on what is unseen, since what is seen is temporary, but what is unseen is eternal.

2 Corinthians 4:18 (NIV)

Many years ago, I worked for a photographer. One of my jobs was to prepare the negatives for the process of developing the photographs. In the negatives, what is dark is actually light on the true photo; what is light on the negative is, in reality, dark. So I became accustomed to thinking 'backwards' to evaluate the negatives.

In the part of the world where I live, we have another kind of backwards thinking: possessions are too highly valued. Many people feel they must have new cars, the latest phones, the biggest televisions and the best homes—whether or not they can afford them. We so often trade our eternal possessions for these fleeting luxuries.

May God forgive us and teach us to use earthly possessions only as a means of glorifying God—to offer hospitality to others, provide for others' needs and act with compassion when we have the opportunity. May God train us to reverse our thinking as we remember that 'what is seen is temporary, but what is unseen is eternal'.

Prayer: *Dear Father, give us vision to see life with your eyes. Amen*

Thought for the day: When we reverse our backwards thinking, we learn to cherish our eternal possessions.

Teri Moffitt (Arkansas, US)

Letting Go

Read Isaiah 46:3–10
The Lord says, 'You… I have… carried since you were born.'
Isaiah 46:3 (NIV)

This year my oldest child will finish school and go to university, and I am not ready to let her go. Despite reminding myself that this is a natural and necessary part of life, I have been struggling to hide my feelings behind a brave and smiling face.

Today I looked out of my window to see an empty bird's nest above my front porch. A month or so ago, I had watched the mother bird build the nest. She diligently sat on her eggs through the cold rains and winds of early spring. Just last week, I saw three baby birds chirping there, waiting to be fed. Now the nest was empty. When did they leave? Where did the time go? How quickly they flew away!

I realise that as my daughter is preparing to leave home we have some similar feelings. Like my daughter, I feel as if I too am flying on wings that are a bit shaky and uncertain. Yet, as I look to God, I am reassured that neither of us faces the unknown alone. In Isaiah, we are reminded that God has carried us from birth, and that he will continue to carry and sustain us even into old age. In knowing this promise I find I am ready to let her go after all.

Prayer: *Dear God, thank you for your promise never to leave us. Because you hold us close, give us the courage to let go when we need to. In Jesus' name. Amen*

Thought for the day: God carries us every moment of our life's journey.

Olive Lois (Kentucky, US)

PRAYER FOCUS: STUDENTS AND THEIR FAMILIES 63

Respect for Nature

Read Genesis 1:29–31

Everything God created is good, and nothing is to be rejected if it is received with thanksgiving.
1 Timothy 4:4 (NIV)

Our bodies need air or we will suffocate; water, or we will dehydrate; and food, or we will starve. Many of us take air, water and food for granted; yet each year we waste and misuse more of the essential natural elements God made for our survival. The materialistic life-style of parts of the world puts a high demand on the earth and damages soil, water, air, food—precisely what God uses to sustain us.

Scripture says that everything God creates is good and is made for our benefit. The first chapter of Genesis describes the global life-support system that he created for us. If we are truly thankful for the gifts he has provided, we will do our part to take care of them. Working hard to care for our rivers and streams to ensure clean drinking water, keeping our air fresh and sweet for breathing and making sure our food is healthy and pure are acts of thanksgiving to our Creator.

Prayer: *Creator God, help us protect and preserve nature because through nature you sustain us. Amen*

Thought for the day: What can I do daily to help protect God's creation?

Stephen J. Bendit (Colorado, US)

Christ's Church

Read 1 Corinthians 12:12–27

In Christ we, though many, form one body, and each member belongs to all the others.
Romans 12:5 (NIV)

When he moved to work in a different city, my son telephoned me to say that he couldn't find a church where he felt comfortable. I realised that he was looking for a church of our denomination, and I explained to him about the living Church of Jesus Christ. I referred him to 1 Corinthians 12:12–27, in which Paul writes about the many parts of the one body of Christ. I encouraged him to read this passage and to worship and enjoy fellowship with others who are part of Christ's body. I reminded him to appreciate the differences among believers in Christ.

Christ is one and there is only one living Church. This living Church of Christ is not about buildings or denominations; rather, it is about fellowship in Jesus' name—'in spirit and in truth' (John 4:24, KJV).

Prayer: *Dear Lord Jesus, we pray for the unity of your Church. Great Redeemer, unite us in your body. Amen*

Thought for the day: 'As members of one body you were called to peace' (Colossians 3:15).

Charlotte Mande Ilunga (Western Cape, South Africa)

A Light for My Path

Read Psalm 119:105–112

Your word is a lamp for my feet, a light on my path.

Psalm 119:105 (NIV)

When members of my family served as missionaries in the Philippines, we lived in an area where the streets were filled with holes. Walking at night without streetlights was treacherous. I asked my mother-in-law, who sent us weekly parcels from home, for a bright torch. The torch arrived, and its beam went far out into the night.

One evening, instead of pointing the beam toward the path on which I was walking, I directed it at the tops of the palm trees overhead. Suddenly, my foot twisted in a hole in the road and I sprawled face down in the dirt. Instead of lighting my pathway, I was playing with the light, with unhappy consequences.

When I picked myself up from the ground, I'd learned an important lesson: I need to point the light, both the torch and the light of God's word, onto my pathway. God's word lights our path only when we read it and apply it to our lives.

Prayer: *Thank you, Lord, for your word that lights our path, revealing the way to follow you. We pray as Jesus taught us, saying, 'Father, hallowed be your name, your kingdom come. Give us each day our daily bread. Forgive us our sins, for we also forgive everyone who sins against us. And lead us not into temptation.'* Amen*

Thought for the day: I will walk in the light of God's word.

Bob Haslam (Tennessee, US)

Perfect Peace

Read Matthew 6:25–34

Do not be anxious about anything, but in every situation, by prayer and petition, with thanksgiving, present your requests to God.
Philippians 4:6 (NIV)

From time to time, each of us can fret and worry, anticipating the worst. However, some of us live in a constant state of anxiety, which can cause us to neglect our health, lose sleep or become depressed—losing the hope of better days.

This isn't what God wants for us. Jesus asked his listeners in Matthew 6:27, 'Can any one of you by worrying add a single hour to your life?' (NIV). Jesus knew that worrying robs us of health, peace, joy and the good that God wants for us.

When I feel the waves of anxiety rise up in me, I immediately focus on the Lord's peace and calm. I pour out my heart to God. The Bible gives me comfort and assurance that he is with me and knows my struggles. I am encouraged to keep trusting and hoping in him. How often must I do this? Every day! It is a continual process.

Isaiah 26:3 says, '[God] you will keep in perfect peace those whose minds are steadfast, because they trust in you'. I am resolved to keep steadfast because I want that peace. Don't we all?

Prayer: *God of compassion, help us to give you our cares and anxieties so we can find peace and rest for our souls. Thank you. Amen*

Thought for the day: Keeping my focus on the Lord gives me clearer vision.

Linda M. Scarola (New York, US)

Quality Work

Read 1 Peter 4:9–11

Whatever you do, work at it with all your heart, as working for the Lord.
Colossians 3:23 (NIV)

I recall as a boy spending summer afternoons in my grandfather's shoe-repair shop. The sounds and images are still vivid in my mind: noisy repair machines, fragments of leather on the floor, busy customers with shoes that had been given a second chance. My grandfather was a man of gentle conviction who took great pride in all he did. This philosophy applied not only to his work but to every aspect of his life. After an encounter with my grandfather, his customers would walk away not only with a pair of newly repaired shoes but also with an inspired and uplifted heart.

I learned an important lesson from my grandfather: our relationship with God requires that we maintain a sense of love and integrity in all that we do, whether it is at work, at school, in the home or in places unfamiliar to us. The manner in which we followers of Jesus Christ perform our responsibilities—even routine tasks—can be an expression of worship and a way of honouring God. Every day provides unique opportunities to minister to those around us. Through our words and actions we can affirm our love of God and our commitment to serve him as good stewards in the world entrusted to us.

Prayer: *O God, may we recognise our true purpose and use the gifts you have given us to honour you. Amen*

Thought for the day: Does my life reflect God's standards?

Robert Miller (Pennsylvania, US)

Miracles: What to do with them

Wouldn't believing be a lot easier if our faith story weren't so intertwined with miracles? For many years I longed to see a miracle, a tiny one, in front of me—just enough to temper my doubts and counter my uncertainties. The disciple Thomas understood. He said, 'Unless I see the mark of the nails in his hands…' (John 20:25). But while he received his miracle by putting his finger in the nail holes, I haven't.

It helped me when I realised that people can be exposed to miracles and never see them. Even participation in a miracle requires faith. Take the Israelites at the Red Sea. Moses was a clever strategist, carefully planning Israel's escape route. He intentionally chose a camp site for the Israelites with their back to the shallow water that scholars identify as the Sea of Reeds. By appearing to be foolishly vulnerable, Moses lured Pharaoh into thinking that his army would capture the defenceless runaways. Then, as scripture describes it, 'the Lord drove the sea back by a strong east wind all night, and turned the sea into dry land' (Exodus 14:21)—and under the cover of darkness, with the gale muffling their movement, Moses led his people across. Seeing what was happening, the shocked Egyptians plunged in, but God 'clogged their chariot wheels so that they turned with difficulty' (14:25). In the ensuing panic, Israel's escape was assured. Moses and the Israelites proceeded to call out to God in thanksgiving. Miracle or coincidence, God or luck—either interpretation involves wagering.

In Tornado Alley in the United States, where I live, there are many curious reports of people and buildings that are miraculously saved. We hear reports of other supposed miracles as well, but what difference does it make? The primal miracles for Jews and Christians are less about breaking natural laws and more about the transformed lives of those who believe in them. What matters about these events is their power to call forth people for the work of liberation and resurrection. For those who believe but do not do, the miracle is no longer miraculous.

The meaning of the Red Sea event lies in the desert living of those for whom the Promised Land hope tints the horizon of their imagination. Resurrection means that our old selves are crucified with Christ so that our new selves may arise from the dead. In the end, the real miracle is faith as a gift. The ability to believe with all one's heart, mind, soul and strength—now that is miraculous.

Question for Reflection

1. How do you compare the miracles in the Bible to the 'miracles' in your own life?

W. Paul Jones is Resident Director of the Hermitage Spiritual Retreat Centre on Lake Pomme de Terre in Southern Missouri. He is a frequent contributor to *Weavings: A Journal of the Christian Spiritual Life* and is the author of twelve books. This prayer workshop is an excerpt from his book *Becoming Who God Wants You to Be: 60 Meditations for Personal Spiritual Direction* published by Upper Room Books in 2013.

Outward Signs

Read Colossians 3:12–17

The fruit of the Spirit is love, joy, peace, patience, kindness, goodness, faithfulness, gentleness and self-control.
Galatians 5:22–23 (CEB)

For the last six years, my husband and I have been teaching in a bilingual school in the north-east part of Thailand. The plain silver cross I wear has given me a connection to Thai Christians, despite the language barrier between us. One heart-warming experience was hearing a voice in the local marketplace say in hesitant English, 'Are you a Christian? I am too. God bless you!' Unexpectedly, I was connected to another person in warm Christian fellowship, which enveloped me and made me thankful for God's goodness and encouragement.

While I was glad to be recognised as a Christian by my cross, I would rather be identified as a follower of Jesus by my actions and by the way I conduct my life. Too often I fail to live up to the teachings of Christ in my everyday life. However, as I study the Bible, pray and follow the leading of the Holy Spirit, I trust that with God's help, I will become more like Jesus and show his love and compassion in my life.

Prayer: *O God of all the world, help us each day to follow your teachings faithfully and to show that we belong to you through the way we live. Amen*

Thought for the day: How do I show God's love to those around me?

Margaret Anne Martin (Otago, New Zealand)

PRAYER FOCUS: THE PEOPLE OF THAILAND   71

Helping Hands

Read 2 Corinthians 9:6–15
I was pushed hard, so that I was falling, but the Lord helped me.
Psalm 118:13 (NRSV)

On 17 April 2013, an explosion at a fertiliser plant destroyed almost half our town in Texas and killed 15 people. Overnight a quiet country town became a town in ruins, with people having no food, water or shelter of any kind. As word of the disaster spread, help came almost immediately from all directions. Bottled water, hot meals and temporary shelter appeared overnight. Volunteers from all over the area came to maintain order, help the injured and clean up debris. The Red Cross set up headquarters for emergency services in the basement of our church, which had sustained damage itself.

However, the cards and letters sent to our town and our church from other towns and churches all over the world were just as important as the other forms of aid we received. Those who wrote these messages of support assured us that we were in their prayers and thoughts daily. This outpouring of love has made the grief easier to bear and the rebuilding more determined. Our town is a living testimony that even in the darkest of disasters, God's people can still shine the light of hope.

Prayer: *Dear Lord, help us never to forget that as long as we have you in our hearts, we are never alone in our problems. Amen*

Thought for the day: When we are at our weakest, God's people give us strength.

Mark A. Carter (Texas, US)

Soul Dust

Read James 1:22–25

'Repent… and turn to God, so that your sins may be wiped out, that times of refreshing may come from the Lord.'
Acts 3:19 (NIV)

I lean back in the recliner, ready to enjoy the rare treat of reading in the afternoon. When I get up to open the window blinds, light floods the room; and I look around in surprise. A layer of dust covers everything. In the darkened room, I did not see the dust; but it was there.

The hidden dust reminded me how I have changed. Before I accepted Jesus as my Saviour, I felt comfortable in ignoring my sins. My communication with God was one-way; I did all the talking and none of the listening. Now I hear from God regularly through reading the Bible, praying or talking with other Christians. I'm glad that Jesus shows me my imperfections through the Holy Spirit and God's teaching, just as light reveals a room's dust. I don't want to miss the intimacy with God or feel the guilt that comes from not dealing with my sins.

When we confess our sins, God forgives us. Gratitude and peace with him replace our uncomfortable feelings of shame and separation. We can welcome seeing our sins. Awareness is a gift, the vital first step in the process of forgiveness that keeps us close to God and banishes guilt.

Prayer: *Dear God, help us to embrace confession as a positive, necessary step toward refreshing our spirits and drawing us close to you. Amen*

Thought for the day: God invites our confessions and offers forgiveness.

Darlene J. Ellis (Oregon, US)

Why Worry So Much?

Read Matthew 6:25–34

God will meet all your needs according to the riches of his glory in Christ Jesus.

Philippians 4:19 (NIV)

A few months ago some stray cats started coming to some of the houses in our neighbourhood. We knew from their constant 'meows' that they were hungry and wanted to be fed. The cats particularly loved fish, so my mother has begun to fry up fish more often than usual.

Thinking about those cats reminds me of our reading for today. The cats do not seem to worry about where their food is coming from, but they still manage to survive. In contrast, I sometimes worry about my future. Financial concerns, health problems and other troubles can cause confusion and stress. But through prayer, Bible study and life's experiences, God teaches me not to worry so much. I am more valuable than cats. Because I am a child of God, I can trust his love and help as I face the future.

Prayer: *Dear Lord, help us to believe that you will love us, help us and guide us throughout our lives. As Jesus taught us, we pray, 'Our Father which art in heaven, Hallowed be thy name. Thy kingdom come. Thy will be done, as in heaven, so in earth. Give us day by day our daily bread. And forgive us our sins; for we also forgive every one that is indebted to us. And lead us not into temptation; but deliver us from evil.'* Amen*

Thought for the day: When God gives abundantly, we can give generously.

Linawati Santoso (East Java, Indonesia)

* Luke 11:2–4 (KJV)

New Life from Dead Wood

Read John 3:1–8
If anyone is in Christ, that person is part of the new creation.
2 Corinthians 5:17 (CEB)

The maple tree beside our front steps had died. Rotten limbs occasionally fell into the street and so we decided to have the tree taken down. The dead wood shattered as it hit the pavement below.

Our neighbour, a woodworking artist, picked up a piece of the dead tree and took it home. A few weeks later, he presented us with a beautiful chalice fashioned out of the dead wood. Prominently displayed in our home, the chalice has become a symbol of what Christ has done for us and what he can do if we allow him to control our lives.

When we have distanced ourselves from the source of life, Christ offers the cup of new life to us. Even when our lives are broken by sin, none of us is beyond redemption in the hands of the master. Christ can take our worst selves and make them productive again. A commitment to him can change our priorities and our attitudes.

Our neighbour created a symbol of our faith from a dead maple tree. From the cross, another tree that is a symbol of death, Christ has offered us new life. 'This cup,' he said, 'is the new covenant by my blood, which is poured out for you' (Luke 22:20).

Prayer: *Eternal God, when we are overwhelmed by temptation or frustrated by doubts, we thank you for the promise of hope. Lift us out of our weakness into the strength of new life we can have in Christ. Amen*

Thought for the day: God makes all things new.

John M. Younginer, Jr (South Carolina, US)

Unselfish Roots

Read Acts 2:42–47
Let us consider how to provoke one another to love and good deeds.
Hebrews 10:24 (NRSV)

One June day, my husband and I decided to visit a nearby histori-cal home. The beautiful house lay nestled behind a long driveway lined with oak trees. My husband and I sat in rocking chairs on the house's veranda and listened to the tour guide share the history of the estate. She then began to talk about the uniqueness of the oak trees. When they are planted together in a row, she said, their roots not only intertwine but fuse together. This interdependent root system allows the oaks to share water and nutrients and to form a stronger hold in the ground. She told us that when a hurricane had swept through that area, their oaks had sustained little damage because they were held strongly together in the earth.

What would happen if Christians held as tightly together through the hurricanes of this life as those oak trees did? What if we poured the strength, wisdom and love that God has rained down on us into the lives of those experiencing hardship? What if we received that same strength, wisdom and love from others when we ourselves are going through trials? God did not design us to live unto ourselves but created us to be a family, firmly bound together by our roots in our Creator.

Prayer: *Dear Lord, help us to hold fast to our family in Christ, freely giving and gratefully receiving. Amen*

Thought for the day: God designed us to support one another through all life's storms.

Emily Bowen (Virginia, US)

Whose Side?

Read Joshua 5:13–15

[Joshua] asked, 'Are you for us or for our enemies?' 'Neither,' [the man] replied, 'but as commander of the army of the Lord I have now come.'
Joshua 5:13–14 (NIV)

The new recruits relaxed in their barracks, talking casually. Suddenly the commander entered. Someone yelled, 'Attention!' Immediately all conversation ceased as the recruits jumped to their feet. The presence of the commanding officer changed their posture and their speech.

Joshua had a similar experience. Near Jericho, he confronted a man who had a sword in his hand. Joshua asked whether he was friend or foe. The man replied that he was neither, but had come as commander of the Lord's army. Immediately Joshua bowed in reverence, asking, 'What message does my Lord have for his servant?' (Joshua 5:14). Joshua's meeting with the commander of the Lord's army changed his posture and his speech.

Sometimes when I'm praying, I think of Joshua. I find myself trying to convince God to be on my side of an issue. Then I realise that prayer is not meant to persuade the Lord to see things my way. Rather, when I meet God in prayer my job is to bow in reverence, aligning my life and my requests with what God wants. After all, Jesus said we are to seek first God's kingdom and his righteousness (see Matthew 6:33).

Prayer: *Blessed Father, help us align our lives with your kingdom and your will. Amen*

Thought for the day: Do my prayers reflect God's priorities?

Marion Speicher Brown (Florida, US)

PRAYER FOCUS: NEW MILITARY RECRUITS   77

Customer Service

Read Philippians 4:4–8

Do not be anxious about anything, but in every situation, by prayer and petition, with thanksgiving, present your requests to God.
Philippians 4:6 (NIV)

'Your call is very important to us,' says the typical customer service recording. When I hear that, I think: 'If it were that important to you, someone would be there to answer!' After discovering how long the wait will be, sometimes I just hang up the phone because what I needed wasn't that important or pressing.

How great it is to contrast that experience with our prayers to God! Sometimes I hear people criticise other people's prayers because they request seemingly unimportant things: for their favourite sports team to win or for the weather to be nice for a day out. Yet, the verse quoted above tells us that there are no unimportant prayers. God can take all these 'calls' at once, encouraging us to call frequently and with any kind of request. We are instructed to take all our concerns to the Lord in prayer, not just the life-or-death ones.

What a marvellous feeling it is to share everything with God: the big, the small and all the things that lie in between!

Prayer: *Dear God, thank you for hearing all the thoughts we bring to you and for loving us unconditionally. Amen*

Thought for the day: My call is very important to God.

Andrew Billings (Alabama, US)

Waves of Peace

Read Isaiah 43:1–7

Thou wilt keep him in perfect peace, whose mind is stayed on thee: because he trusteth in thee.
Isaiah 26:3 (KJV)

Life had become complicated. Starting a new job and caring for my three children was hard enough, but one of my parents was ill and my brother also needed my help. I was exhausted from travelling from place to place. I needed a break. The sea has always calmed me, so I drove to the beach. Strolling along the water's edge, I soaked in the peacefulness of the moment. The gentle rhythm of the waves soothed my stress. My anxieties evaporated in the breeze and I felt carefree and light. I wanted the moment to last for ever.

I left the beach determined to hold on to my sense of peace. I thanked God for my blessings and my difficulties. When I was overwhelmed, I prayed. God was my hiding place, and I trusted him to help me. My troubles didn't disappear, but as I continued to pray my stress was replaced by peace.

I used to think I could be at peace only in the absence of problems, but God doesn't promise a life free of stress. He promises peace in the midst of our troubles. Even though our circumstances may not change, our response to them can change. When we give our problems to God, peace washes over us like gentle ocean waves.

Prayer: *Thank you, God, for helping us with the challenges of life. With each prayer, may we exhale our worries and inhale your peace. Amen*

Thought for the day: Peace is just a prayer away.

Doris Hoover (Florida, US)

Good Sorts

Read Romans 15:1–6

May the God of steadfastness and encouragement grant you to live in harmony with one another, in accordance with Christ Jesus.
Romans 15:5 (NRSV)

Almost all the news I read in the daily newspaper and magazines or watch on television is depressing—disasters, broken marriages, crime and conflict all over the world.

Recently, however, I have found more encouraging stories, entitled 'Good Sorts', appearing in our New Zealand newspapers and on television. The stories feature people who do amazing and uplifting things over their lifetime: bringing hope, support and opportunities to people in need—mostly without any personal financial gain.

These uplifting stories remind me of Christ's model. By acknowledging the need for more of us to be givers rather than simply takers, we can help the world to become a more loving and caring place.

Our faith calls us to bring joy to others, helping them to have a more fulfilling life. Every day as we walk through life we can extend friendship to the people we meet. We can greet them, smile and be pleased to see them. We all have the potential to be 'Good Sorts' by passing on God's love to those we meet.

Prayer: *Loving God, you enrich our lives with your love and compassion. Help us to show that love to others in all we do. Amen*

Thought for the day: Today I will follow Christ's example and show love to those I meet.

Margaret Gordon (Auckland, New Zealand)

In our Darkest Hours

Read Psalm 27:1–5
The Lord is my light and my salvation—whom shall I fear?
Psalm 27:1 (NIV)

The night was sultry, humid. Overhead, a flash of lightning preceded a thunderclap. Petrified, my dog leapt on to my bed, shaking with fear. As she trembled and tried to burrow under the bedclothes, I resigned myself to a sleepless night. Frustrated through lack of sleep, in the early hours of the morning I padded downstairs.

As my fingers groped for the light switch a sudden flash extinguished the light. I unearthed a candle and matches and soon mended the fuse, musing on how helpless we feel when a storm puts out the lights.

I remembered my childhood in Sunday school, how eagerly I had listened to the story of Jesus and the disciples in a boat on the Sea of Galilee when a storm arose. My mind went back to Jesus' wonderful words: 'Peace, be still.' And everything became calm.

Jesus is ever present. He's the light in our darkest hours. When all else fails, in the midst of our storms, we can rely on him to restore our peace.

Prayer: *Lord, when life's storms are raging and the light of life goes out, bring us your peace. Amen*

Thought for the day: In my darkest hour I will remember that Jesus is with me.

Pauline Pullan (Yorkshire, England)

The House of God

Read 1 Corinthians 6:19–20

I am writing you these instructions so that... you will know how people ought to conduct themselves in God's household, which is the church of the living God, the pillar and foundation of the truth.
1 Timothy 3:14–15 (NIV)

Our text reminds me of a time when I was in the army and enjoying a three-day pass in Germany. We were doing some sightseeing, and our group stopped to visit a very old and beautiful church. It was massive, and as we entered, I immediately experienced a sense of awe and reverence, a feeling which was quickly reinforced when a man motioned for me to take off my hat.

Is today's quoted verse teaching us to be on our best behaviour only while inside a church building? Is it the building that is the 'pillar and foundation' of God's truth, or something else? Although our church buildings are symbols of the household of God, our bodies are also his dwelling place as the pillars of the church (see today's reading and Revelation 3:12).

My visit to the church in Germany reminded me that I am always in church because my body is God's temple. If we are walking faithfully with Christ, we will reflect that holiness in our speech, our love, our faith, our purity—wherever we are.

Prayer: *O God, we long to be your holy people in every step of our life's journey. Amen*

Thought for the day: I am in the household of God no matter where I am.

Timothy James Wendt (South Dakota, US)

God's Presence Brings Joy

Read Psalm 16:5–11
You will fill me with joy in your presence.
Psalm 16:11 (NIV)

Today's technology blesses us as long-distance grandparents. My husband and I delight in conversations with our young grandchildren using computers and smart phones. During a live-screen computer visit, we can read picture books together, watch as they get their hair shampooed, laugh as they play games and even share in bedtime prayers.

Enjoying these interactions with our grandchildren makes me think about how much more God enjoys interacting with us. When we read and reflect on scripture, take part in Christian fellowship, serve those in need and pray regularly, we draw near to God. More than focusing on activities or works, he values our desire to spend time in his presence. He asks us simply to come and rest in that presence.

I'm thankful that God is with us in all circumstances. When I walk through a colourful, fragrant garden, I find joy in thanking God. While I care for an ill family member, he is present. Even as I grieve, I call out to him to be my strength, hope and comfort. The psalmist wrote, 'Let the righteous be glad and celebrate before God. Let them rejoice with gladness!' (Psalm 68:3, CEB).

Prayer: *Dear God, thank you for creating us for relationship with you. Your presence with us is a gift beyond measure. Amen*

Thought for the day: Being in God's presence brings joy.

Jane A. Compton (Oregon, US)

Sowing and Reaping

Read John 13:34–35

You reap whatever you sow.
Galatians 6:7 (NRSV)

Getting to know our neighbours can be an adventure. Across the street lives a lovely 91-year-old lady, a widow, who is almost totally blind. The first time we talked, she ended our visit saying, 'God bless you.' My ears perked up. Later, she told me she was a Christian but she didn't go to church because of her lack of sight. She is also unsteady on her feet from sciatica and other problems with walking, so being in crowds is dangerous for her. I offered to visit her once a week and read to her from the Bible. I wanted to help fill the void left by her inability to attend church.

I'm not sure now whether God opened the door so that I could minister to her or so that she could to minister to me. I read scripture to her, but her positive attitude and love of the Lord have become an inspiration to me. When she found out that I write Christian literature, she asked me to read some to her. She always responds with encouragement or a challenge.

God took a situation I thought was for my neighbour's good and brought joy to both her and me. How blessed we are that God makes all things work together for good for those who love the Lord (see Romans 8:28).

Prayer: *Thank you, dear God, for the many ways you bring peace, joy and a sense of purpose to our lives. Amen*

Thought for the day: God calls us to invest in relationships with our neighbours.

Shirley McCoy (Florida, US)

Man in the Tower

Read Proverbs 2:1–11

In all your ways submit to [the Lord], and he will make your paths straight.
Proverbs 3:6 (NIV)

When my children were younger, they looked forward to the challenge of a large maze which was organised at a local farm. Each year, the design of the maze was different. One year we took much longer than usual to find the exit, repeatedly encountering dead ends. My son began to worry that we were not going to be able to get out. A short time later, he pointed to a tall wooden tower not far away at the top of which stood a young man with binoculars. 'Let's ask him!' exclaimed my son.

Our lives are not unlike a large maze, requiring us to make many choices and decisions. We may begin our life's journey with a false sense of confidence in our own ability to navigate—only to discover the dead ends of failed relationships, unforeseen career changes, betrayal or illness. Times like these require us to retrace our steps and turn to Christ who can heal our pain and renew our strength to press on toward joyful living. When we are lost, we can look to Jesus, the 'man in the tower' always on watch, and say, 'Show me the way!'

Prayer: *Gracious God, when the road we walk seems dark, confusing and hopeless, grant us the courage to press on toward the eternal reward you promise for each of us. Amen*

Thought for the day: When our life comes to a dead end, Jesus shows us the way out.

Robert C. Miller (Pennsylvania, US)

Our Family, God's Family

Read 1 Thessalonians 5:16–18

Their delight is in the law of the Lord, and on his law they meditate day and night.

Psalm 1:2 (NRSV)

Every morning I get up early enough to read the Bible and *The Upper Room*. It is a good start to my day, and as I read the Bible passage and the meditation, I reflect on the writer and where in the world they are from. In doing so, I feel I am a part of the large family of God.

Some of my family in different places have already read the day's Bible passage and meditation, have thought about it and prayed; now it's my turn. In my prayers I include the writer of the meditation. Later, other people will read and pray, making a continuous chain of prayer and blessing encompassing the world. If a line could be drawn from reader to writer all around the world, lines would criss-cross the globe across various time zones, and we would have 24 hours of prayer flooding the world every day.

What an encouraging thought—we all play a small part in the large family of God.

Prayer: *Father, hear us as we pray and meditate on your word each day. Amen*

Thought for the day: I am part of the worldwide family of God.

Brian Gaunt (Yorkshire, England))

True Greatness

Read Matthew 18:1–5

The disciples came to Jesus and asked, 'Who, then, is greatest in the kingdom of heaven?'
Matthew 18:1 (NIV)

The disciples were disputing the issue of greatness in the kingdom of heaven. In one sense, their debate was admirable. It revealed their belief in the promises of Jesus and his glorious kingdom. But when they posed the question, Jesus rebuked them saying, 'Unless you change and become like little children, you will never enter the kingdom of heaven' (Matthew 18:3). The disciples needed to turn in a new direction, to get rid of pride and to replace it with a childlike spirit of trust, dependence and humility. Only then would they be great.

People today love to debate who will go down in history as the greatest president or prime minister. Sports commentators enjoy discussing the greatest all-time sports figures. Although human achievements, wisdom and power are impressive in our world, none of them has anything to do with greatness from Jesus' perspective. Selflessness, humility, compassion and love identify greatness in the kingdom of God.

Prayer: *Dear Lord, may our Christian walk be characterised by greatness from your perspective. Amen*

Thought for the day: When I humble myself as a child, I can do great works in God's kingdom.

Geraldine Nicholas (Alberta, Canada)

Never Out of Season

Read Ecclesiastes 3:1–8
For everything there is a season, and a time for every matter under heaven.
Ecclesiastes 3:1 (NRSV)

During a three-hour period one afternoon, I conducted both a funeral and a wedding. The contrast between these two events was marked. In the first service we gathered at a graveside to remember an earthly life that had come to an end. At the second service we stood at an altar to celebrate the beginning of a new life in marriage.

While each event represented a distinct season of life, they shared common ground in the love of God. At the funeral we rejoiced in the victory we have over death because of Jesus' crucifixion and resurrection. Paul writes, 'God shows his love for us because while we were still sinners, Christ died for us' (Romans 5:8, CEB). We thanked a loving God for giving us new life in Jesus Christ. During the wedding, we were reminded that marriage is a gift from God, and we focused on 1 Corinthians 13, which describes Christian love and its permanence.

In Romans 8:38, Paul reminds us that 'nothing can separate us from God's love in Christ Jesus our Lord' (CEB). No matter the season of life we face, we can always count on the love of God.

Prayer: *Dear God, help us to remember that you love us and remain with us through every period of our lives. Amen*

Thought for the day: God's love can transform every season of our lives.

Bryan Taylor (Indiana, US)

Small but Worthwhile

Read Ephesians 4:25–32

Let the favour of the Lord our God be upon us, and prosper for us the work of our hands.

Psalm 90:17 (NRSV)

'What did your hands do today?' One day I came across that question in a devotional book. When I paused to ponder my answer, I realised that what I was doing with my hands was small but worthwhile. On Mondays I go to church and take apart the large church flower arrangement from the Sunday services to make small bouquets for sick, elderly or lonely members. I spend a few hours sorting the flowers and rearranging them. Then someone else distributes them.

Although my work is a small effort, I know it spreads joy and love to people who often feel forgotten. We all have a need to be noticed and acknowledged. We all have a need for someone to say we count, especially when things are not going so well in our lives. That's what I am trying to do. We can each do something to brighten another's day. All it takes is the power of our loving imagination and the work of our hands.

Prayer: *Dear God, help us to serve you and share your love, giving new life and hope to others. Amen*

Thought for the day: Whatever I do, I can work at it with all my heart, as though I were working for the Lord (see Colossians 3:23).

Chris Driver (Gautang, South Africa)

Glass or Diamonds?

Read Mark 10:17–27
'Where your treasure is, there your heart will be also.'
Matthew 6:21 (NIV)

I always enjoy visiting a castle not far from where I live, which dates from the 13th century. Visitors can walk at leisure through well-preserved rooms to admire the pictures and paintings. The last, and best, room of all features a large collection of valuable china and intricate needlework displays.

Recently I spent a whole morning in this room, gazing at each exhibit. What a joy! As I did so most other visitors merely paused to give the collection a quick glance and then headed for the gift shop next door, eager to buy souvenirs. I felt sad that they had missed out on a chance to delight in such exquisite craftsmanship, although now and then a visitor did stop long enough for us to share admiring comments.

On the way home I realised that the morning had been a real-life parable. It's so easy to miss out on the immensely valuable gifts which Jesus longs to give us because we prefer to find temporary pleasures elsewhere; like opting for glass when we could have diamonds.

Prayer: *Lord Jesus, help us not to miss out on all that you long to give us today. Amen*

Thought for the day: I wonder what treasures I'll discover in Jesus today.

Elaine Brown (Perthshire, Scotland)

God's Healing Touch

Read Psalm 71:17–22

Though you have made me see troubles, many and bitter, you will restore my life again.

Psalm 71:20 (NIV)

Following my mother's operation, I returned to work. I thought her recovery was certain. The next day I learned that she had woken up and asked for me. But before I could return to her, she unexpectedly slipped into a coma and never woke up. We didn't get to share a last conversation or reminisce about the blessings of our life together and talk about our hopes for the future. I was crushed. I was shocked. I was angry.

We are often told that time will heal grief, but how and with whom we spend our time makes a difference in our healing. Through prayer and reading God's word, I was able to find direction, strength and hope in dealing with the pain of my mother's death. Talking with others who had experienced similar pain also brought comfort. I have also found that living in ways that honour my mother is helpful and meaningful. This practice has placed her in a healthy, wonderful place in my heart. Thanks to God and faithful friends, my wounds have healed.

Prayer: *Dear Father, thank you for providing us with peace in our grief. We seek to be filled with your Spirit always. Amen*

Thought for the day: Time with God heals.

Veneal Williams (South Carolina, US)

Hard to Love

Read John 15:1–17

'If you love those who love you, what credit is that to you? For even sinners love those who love them.'
Luke 6:32 (NRSV)

Jesus teaches his disciples how to live. In John 15:1–9, he uses the image of a vine and its branches to show his followers the importance of abiding in him and allowing him to live through them. In John 15:10–17, Jesus commands his disciples to love one another and to be willing to lay down their lives for one another. His command to us is the same.

Loving those who love us is easy. We gladly sacrifice our own needs and wants for the sake of those we love and care about: our spouses, children, grandchildren and friends.

What about people we don't love? What about people whose words and actions make loving them difficult? How do we lay down our lives for those who are not our friends or for those who have hurt us with cruel words and actions?

I have come to believe that setting aside our anger, hurt and indifference and praying daily for those who have hurt us is one way of laying down our lives for them. This practice allows God to grace us with the ability to show them kindness. Asking God to show us our part, our responsibilities to him and to other people, may be the catalyst needed to restore broken relationships and to strengthen our resolve to serve God in all that we do.

Prayer: *Dear Lord Jesus, help us to show your love in all that we say and do. In your name, we pray. Amen*

Thought for the day: Today I will pray for someone I don't usually pray for.

Patricia Wilgis-Patton (Texas, US)

Echoes to Come

Read Matthew 7:7–11

'Seek first [God's] kingdom and his righteousness, and all these things will be given to you as well.'
Matthew 6:33 (NIV)

During a recent trip, my husband Tim and I couldn't resist calling across the canyon that lay before us. We were delighted to hear our voices echo back. This reminded me of the joy I feel when God's word is regularly repeated in my heart and I apply it to every part of my life. With this in mind, Tim and I invited a group of Christian friends to pray words of hope and faith for our business. We wrote down the Bible verses and key ideas that we prayed, including Matthew 6:33.

But later, when our business slowed, we began to lose confidence. We looked for direction in the media and listened to reports of companies closing as though we no longer believed God's promise to sustain our basic needs. Then, finally realising that once again we needed wisdom and God's perspective, we went back and revisited the truths in scripture, such as Jesus' words in Matthew 7:7–11. We found that rereading pages of our spiritual journals or speaking with friends about God's faithfulness in the past deepened our trust.

When we remember God's promises, we refresh our thoughts with hope. When we fully trust in God's word to sustain us we can capture the steadfast love that belongs to us.

Prayer: *Loving Father, remind us of what you said yesterday so that we can draw strength from it today. Amen*

Thought for the day: When we read scripture often, we find fresh hope in God's promises.

Lynn Hare (Oregon, US)

'Go Back'

Read James 2:14–20

Someone will say, 'You have faith; I have deeds.' Show me your faith without deeds, and I will show you my faith by my deeds.
James 2:18 (NIV)

One rainy day when I was driving home from having visited my sister, I passed a man walking with a backpack. As I drove further down the road, I heard an inner voice say, 'Go back and give him a lift.' I felt as if God was talking to me. So I turned around and gave the man a lift.

In our conversation, I found out that the man was walking from Washington, DC to Florida to meet his brother. After some thought, I decided to go to the bus station and buy him a ticket to Florida. As I gave him the ticket, I said, 'May God bless you.' Driving home, I realised that God had blessed me by giving me the opportunity to help someone in need.

Prayer: *Dear Lord, challenge us always to be willing to help those in need and thereby reveal the love Christ has for all of us. We pray as Jesus taught us, saying, 'Our Father which art in heaven, Hallowed be thy name. Thy kingdom come. Thy will be done in earth, as it is in heaven. Give us this day our daily bread. And forgive us our debts, as we forgive our debtors. And lead us not into temptation, but deliver us from evil: For thine is the kingdom, and the power, and the glory, for ever.'* Amen*

Thought for the day: When God speaks, I will listen—and prepare to be surprised!

Paul Alton Basilico (Georgia, US)

        * Matthew 6:9–13 (KJV)

My Toys

Read Jeremiah 9:23–24

This is eternal life: that they know you, the only true God, and Jesus Christ, whom you have sent.
John 17:3 (NIV)

When I was a child, I was proud of my toy car collection. I loved showing off my latest little metal car to my friends. When I grew up, I thought I was beyond childish behaviour. I was wrong. As an adult, I found different reasons to show off: weight loss, musical talents, advanced degrees, a measure of fame. My toys were not tiny cars, but real cars that were loud, red and fast.

Jeremiah 9:23–24 brought me up short. What should I be proud of? I should be proud not of what I have but of whom I know. I can boast not of my own intellect but of my understanding of God's character, which leads to faithful love and justice for all of us who do not deserve it and righteousness for all of us who cannot earn it.

I realised that my little metal cars and all my toys would eventually turn to rust. But by talking to God and learning about him in the Bible, I could have a relationship with him, who made everything in the universe. Instead of showing off my toy cars, I can show off my God and his great love.

Prayer: *Dear God, make us aware of your greatness and make us proud to call you our God and our friend. Amen*

Thought for the day: I can take pride in my God.

Tom Fuller (Oregon, US)

SUNDAY 26 JULY

Letting Go

Read Deuteronomy 31:1–8

It is the Lord who goes before you. He will be with you; he will not fail you or forsake you. Do not fear or be dismayed.
Deuteronomy 31:8 (NRSV)

Several years ago when I changed jobs and moved to a new city, I left behind my young-adult sons. I also said goodbye to many friends I had made over the years. As I was embracing my new surroundings, I was diagnosed with cancer. My health changed dramatically, and my world turned upside down. These changes challenged me, but everyone experiences change.

As Christ-followers our journey of embracing and letting go is grounded in God's eternal love, grace and mercy. Sometimes segments of this journey are long and arduous; sometimes they are brief and joyful. The freedom to embrace and to let go is a gift from God.

No matter where we are on our journey, God is with us. Perhaps we are welcoming new friends and family. Some of us may be changing vocations and moving to new places. Others are learning to accept unexpected health issues or the loss of loved ones.

Today I am thankful for God's faithful presence in life's changes, both joyful and difficult. As we accept life's transitions, we make room for something new—a more loving heart, trusting spirit and peaceful soul.

Prayer: *Journeying God, help us to embrace your faithfulness in times of transition and change. Amen*

Thought for the day: Letting go is always rooted in God's love, grace and mercy.

Sandi Marr (Ontario, Canada)

Gathering Fruit

Read Galatians 5:22–25

God said, 'I give you every seed-bearing plant on the face of the whole earth and every tree that has fruit with seed in it. They will be yours for food.'
Genesis 1:29 (NIV)

I am a member of a Christian Friendship Fellowship group. Once a year we spend several days together at Pitlochry, a little town situated at the heart of the Scottish Highlands. We study scriptural themes, walk, socialise and explore the surrounding countryside. On our last visit the theme was 'The fruits of the Spirit'.

Our study sessions, together with our visits to places of scenic beauty, reminded us of God's goodness. As we passed fields, farmers were harvesting their crops. Along the riverbanks, anglers were fishing for salmon. Blackberries were ready for picking; market gardeners and their staff were harvesting them.

Yes, God provides us with many good things. However, to make use of his gifts, we have to gather them in. The same is true of the gifts of the Spirit. They are freely given, but to realise them, we have to make a conscious effort to incorporate them into our lives.

Prayer: *Thank you, Lord, for all your gifts. Guide us as we seek to harvest our spiritual gifts also. Amen*

Thought for the day: Today I will be aware of God's goodness all around me.

William Findlay (Scotland)

PRAYER FOCUS: THOSE SEEKING GOD'S GIFTS

No Words Needed

Read Psalm 139:1-6
Even before a word is on my tongue, O Lord, you know it completely.
Psalm 139:4 (NRSV)

One of my cousins and I have cabins near each other in a Norwegian forest. Every summer both she and I receive visits from our grandchildren. Her grandchildren are English and do not know how to speak or understand Norwegian. Last summer English-speaking Minna was playing with Norwegian-speaking Lyder. Minna was pretending to speak Norwegian, and Lyder was answering in what he thought was English. They were two and three years old and seemed to have no problem understanding each other.

The incident made me think about my prayer life. I often find that I lack the proper words, or I am uncertain about how to express myself to the Lord. The 'conversation' between Minna and Lyder helped me understand that God does not need to be addressed in any particular way in order to know what fills our hearts. Paul puts it this way: 'Likewise the Spirit helps us in our weakness; for we do not know how to pray as we ought, but that very Spirit intercedes with sighs too deep for words' (Romans 8:26). We do not need to be eloquent in speech to gain God's love and compassion.

Prayer: *Dear Lord, thank you for listening to us even before our words or thoughts are formed. Amen*

Thought for the day: Even when I cannot find the proper words, God understands my prayers.

Øystein Brinch (Oslo, Norway)

Seeing with New Eyes

Read Ephesians 1:15–20

Brothers and sisters, whatever is true, whatever is noble, whatever is right, whatever is pure, whatever is lovely, whatever is admirable—if anything is excellent or praiseworthy—think about such things.
Philippians 4:8 (NIV)

Several years ago, I wanted to adopt a more positive attitude in life. Remembering Philippians 4:8 I thought it might help to memorise the verse and try to follow its teaching. But the task still felt overwhelming.

Then I realised I could break down the verse into smaller phrases and focus on one virtue each day. On Monday, I began. If I started to think negatively, I repeated to myself, 'Whatever is true, think on these things', and I focused on various verses in the Bible since they reveal God's truths. The process invigorated and energised me.

On Tuesday, I thought about 'whatever is noble' and focused on the selfless acts of others. Thinking about 'whatever is right' on Wednesday helped me to make better choices. On Thursday, as I thought about 'whatever is pure', I often reflected on the love of my mother and my mother-in-law.

Thinking about 'whatever is lovely' on Friday led me to look for beauty. To help me think about 'whatever is admirable' on Saturday, I looked for the best in other people. Sunday's thought, 'if anything is excellent or praiseworthy', summed up the whole week, and I searched for the good in all situations and in all people.

Throughout this process, I began to see with new eyes and to appreciate the goodness of God that surrounds me.

Prayer: *Dear God, thank you for helping us see through your eyes. Amen*

Thought for the day: The Bible can help us see through God's eyes.

Delores Harmon Kight (Florida, US)

Untold Blessings

Read Philippians 2:1–4
God sets the lonely in families.
Psalm 68:6 (NIV)

On 6 October 2011, a meditation I had written was published in *The Upper Room*. I described my life as a single, childless woman, who struggles with feelings of loneliness and purposelessness. After reading it a woman named Doris contacted me. She wanted to tell me that the meditation had encouraged her because she struggles with the feelings I had written about.

Although we live hundreds of miles apart and there is almost a 30-year difference in our ages, Doris and I have become good friends. We maintain weekly contact through emails and other correspondence.

Our friendship started because my meditation blessed Doris. But since then, I have been the recipient of untold blessings from our relationship. She steadfastly prays for me and offers me encouragement. We both find comfort in knowing that we are praying for each other and that we are not alone in our struggles.

God has wonderful ways of meeting our needs. I find it amazing that he connected Doris and me. What a joy it is that we serve a God who knows our deepest needs and takes joy in meeting these needs—often in beautiful and unexpected ways!

Prayer: *Dear God, thank you for the gift of friendship. Help us to be the face of Christ both to our current friends and to friends we have yet to meet. Amen*

Thought for the day: God blesses us in unexpected ways.

Mary McKheen (Michigan, US)

Dealing with Distractions

Read Luke 10:38–42

The Lord [said,] 'Martha, Martha, you are worried and distracted by many things. One thing is necessary. Mary has chosen the better part. It won't be taken away from her.'

Luke 10:41–42 (CEB)

Lately I've been finding myself bombarded by emails, text messages, calendar reminders and Facebook requests. I thought the smartphone was supposed to make my life more manageable or at least more fun to manage. But the more often I use my phone, the less I can enjoy face-to-face conversations. I find myself answering emails while I'm eating lunch. I used to gaze at the rose bushes and the sunflowers that grow in my garden. Now I stare at a four-inch screen so that I can be even more efficient at work. If I have some free time, I use it to schedule more reminders of things to do or I flip through countless apps. I am more distracted than Martha. At least she spent her time preparing to serve a meal for Jesus. What excuse can I offer?

I need to hear the story of Mary and Martha. I need to slow down, to listen and to focus on Jesus. Worrying has no reward in heaven. Rushing to get everything done keeps me from building life-restoring relationships. Mary had the right idea. Putting everything on hold to be with Jesus is 'the better part'.

Prayer: *Patient God, teach us how to focus on you so that we listen more and worry less. Amen*

Thought for the day: Today I will slow down and listen for a word from Jesus.

David W. Poe (Missouri, US)

PRAYER FOCUS: WORKAHOLICS

A Positive Attitude

Read Deuteronomy 3:21–28

Encourage one another and build each other up.

1 Thessalonians 5:11 (NIV)

A new member joined the staff of the European Bible Institute. This young colleague was gifted and outgoing, and she would eventually take over some of my responsibilities. I found myself confronted with a choice: I could become bitter and jealous or I could adopt a positive attitude.

While I was reading Deuteronomy 3, the Lord drew my attention to God's exhortation to Moses concerning Joshua, his successor: 'Encourage and strengthen him' (Deuteronomy 3:28). This was God's personal word to me: encourage my new colleague—even more, point out her strong points to the boss. With the Lord's help and grace I decided to support this colleague, who is now also a friend.

I needed the help of the Lord to keep encouraging her, especially when she was given some of the responsibilities I really enjoyed. One way the Lord has encouraged me is through scripture: 'I know that good itself does not dwell… in my sinful nature. For I have the desire to do what is good, but I cannot carry it out' (Romans 7:18). I am grateful for my Lord who works in us all through the Spirit 'to will and to act in order to fulfil his good purpose' (Philippians 2:13).

Prayer: *Thank you, Lord, for the relevance of your word in our lives day by day. Help us to immerse ourselves in scripture so that we can hear you speaking to us. Amen*

Thought for the day: God blesses us when we encourage others.

Ruth Nussbaumer (Alsace, France)

Trials with Purpose

Read 2 Corinthians 1:3–7

[God] consoles us in all our affliction, so that we may be able to console those who are in any affliction with the consolation with which we ourselves are consoled by God.
2 Corinthians 1:4 (NRSV)

My mother was taken to hospital with a blood clot in her lungs. I remember her struggling to breathe and wondering if each breath would be her last. She was lucky to be alive as this condition was usually fatal. But with proper medical care she continued to improve and eventually was able to go home. I was grateful to God for helping her recover and for helping me cope with the fear of losing her.

Two months later, I went to the home of Barbara, an elderly woman whom I often took to church on Sundays. When she answered the door, she was pale and having difficulty breathing. I recognised in her my mother's symptoms. Barbara tried to send me on my way, but I insisted that we call for an ambulance. The paramedics rushed her to hospital where she was diagnosed with a blood clot in her lung. As she recovered, the doctor told her that had she not received immediate medical care, she would have died.

I am thankful that the difficult experience of watching my mother's health problem enabled me to help Barbara. In spite of the trials we sometimes endure, we can trust that God is working to bring good from every situation.

Prayer: *Dear Lord Jesus, help us use our past pains to help others through their trials. Amen*

Thought for the day: God is working for good in every situation.

John Bagdanov (California, US)

Moved with Compassion

Read Matthew 9:35–38
When [Jesus] saw the crowds, he had compassion on them, because they were harassed and helpless, like sheep without a shepherd.
Matthew 9:36 (NIV)

Scrunched in the seat of a pedal rickshaw in India, I observed the masses of humanity pressed together on the narrow street. The sound of horns, the smell of fumes and the sight of chaotic bustling overwhelmed my senses. Struck by the scene, I wondered what God thought while looking at such a crowd. Then I thought of Matthew 9:36: 'When Jesus saw the crowd, he had compassion on them.'

Jesus' response to the people revealed the vision of God. The word 'compassion' in Greek indicates a gut-wrenching burden for people. That burden led Jesus to send his followers on a mission to engage the 'harassed and helpless'. Jesus wanted his followers to reach those who are suffering.

Viewing this crowd of people has led me to pray for them and moved me to deep compassion. I was propelled into action. As our rickshaw slowly manoeuvred its way through the crowds, I wondered what our world would be like if every Christ-follower were to pray for those who are suffering and then to act with compassion as Jesus commands.

Prayer: *Dear Jesus, give us a compassion that moves us to see others through your eyes. Send us to serve those who are suffering. Amen*

Thought for the day: I want to see the world through God's eyes of compassion.

Leslie Anne Neal Segraves (Tennessee, US)

A New Start

Read 1 John 1:5–9

If we confess our sins, he who is faithful and just will forgive us our sins and cleanse us from all unrighteousness.
1 John 1:9 (NRSV)

As part of our retirement plan, my wife and I are building a new home. In the first step of the process, the construction crew removed large amounts of debris—including trees, vines, roots and all sorts of clutter. As a result, the area was clean and prepared for the new construction.

I began to compare this process to my own life. God promises to clear my life by removing the trees of sin, the vines of doubt, the roots of unworthy living and all of the clutter that had led me to make poor choices.

As I looked at the freshly cleaned ground, ready for a new use, I thanked God for making our lives clean and free of all that stands in the way of trust and obedience. To anyone willing to accept his offer of redemption, God promises a new life and a rewarding relationship. I have learned that it is never too late to respond to God's invitations. He will continue to knock on the door to our hearts until we make the choice to open it and let him enter (see Matthew 7:7; Luke 11:9; Revelation 3:20).

Prayer *Heavenly Father, help us to remove everything that stands in the way of responding to your offer of a relationship with us. We pray in Jesus' name. Amen*

Thought for the day: God can cleanse any life.

James W. (Skip) Cox (North Carolina, US)

Like a Child

Read Luke 21:1–4

[Jesus] called a child, whom he put among them, and said, 'Truly I tell you, unless you change and become like children, you will never enter the kingdom of heaven.'
Matthew 18:2–3 (NRSV)

Recently my son David realised that we would no longer have any-where to live because our landlord had asked us to move out imme-diately. With a serious expression, David came to me and said, 'Daddy, I have a piggy bank, and there is a lot of change there. I will give everything to you. You can rent a new flat, and we can live there.' I thanked him and embraced him, but told him that his money was not enough; we needed much more. David responded, 'I will find more. I will look where my toys are. Somewhere there will be more coins, and I will give all of them to you.' I embraced him and wept.

When Jesus calls us to be like children, he has precisely such qualities in mind: a sincere faith, sacrifice without the slightest greed and unselfish love. After all, even if I scold my son, he still stretches out a hand to me and runs to embrace me, looking for forgiveness and love. This is an example for us to follow as children of a heavenly Father. I think this is what Jesus was teaching through his story about the widow's gift to the temple. Such sacrificial giving is the means by which the Church is built and sustained.

Prayer: *Dear God, our Father, help us to realise that everything we have in this life comes from you. Help us to be sacrificial as we give to your Church and to those in need. Amen*

Thought for the day: God is amazingly generous to the generous.

Pavel Serdukov (Moscow, Russia)

Guarantee

Read Ephesians 1:11–14

Be filled with courage and be drawn together in love, and so have the full wealth of assurance which true understanding brings.
Colossians 2:2 (GNB)

When you buy a loaf of bread, you might get a receipt, but not a guarantee. If you buy a washing machine, TV or car, you hope to get both.

What happens if you decide to 'buy into' Jesus? Is there a guarantee that comes with him? God loves us so much that he gave Jesus as a gift. We don't have to 'buy into' Jesus; indeed, we can't. It was Jesus who 'bought' us. And the price was his death on the cross. He bought us freedom from our wrongdoing, and in accepting God's gift we are reconciled to him through Jesus.

Where is the guarantee that this is for real? The resurrection of Jesus is one guarantee—when he defeated sin and death. The second guarantee is the Holy Spirit, whom Paul writes about to the Ephesians. The guarantee comes with a promise, giving us assurance.

Whether we are starting to ask about the Christian faith, or we have already begun our walk of faith with Jesus, we are all learners. We move forward together, aware of our weaknesses and limited understanding, but with the assurance of God's loving presence to encourage us.

Prayer: *Thank you, God, for our Saviour Jesus Christ, and for the comforting presence of the Spirit in our lives. Amen*

Thought for the day: To appreciate the immensity of what God has done for us.

Pam Pointer (Wiltshire, England)

Jolly Hard Work!

Read 1 John 4:7–12

You were called to freedom, brothers and sisters; only don't let this freedom be an opportunity to indulge your selfish impulses, but serve each other through love.

Galatians 5:13 (CEB)

This has been a difficult year for farmers in Australia. After experiencing at least seven years of drought, many of us have faced a series of floods that have destroyed fences and devastated crops and livestock. Recently, a group of people came from a sister church in Sydney, some 750 kilometres away, to give us a hand with our clean-up. We were feeling overwhelmed with the work ahead; then they arrived and began to drag fences out of the mud and re-erect the posts and wire. It was a messy job and jolly hard work! The fact that they took a week off to come and help us was mind-boggling. By the time they left we felt that we would make it through. We didn't even know these people, yet they came and demonstrated God's love to us.

We don't have to travel to far-off places to do something for God. Sometimes he calls us to care for people in or near our own neighbourhoods.

Prayer: *Loving God, thank you for your people who are willing to do whatever it takes to love and serve you by loving and serving others. Amen*

Thought for the day: We can be agents of God's saving love.

Janine Randell (New South Wales, Australia)

Representing Jesus Well

Read Romans 5:1–5

You need endurance, so that when you have done the will of God, you may receive what was promised.
Hebrews 10:36 (NRSV)

Recently, I was reminded of my inability to sew when attempting to return a button to its rightful place on my shirt. The thread fought with the eye of the needle. The button slipped around like soft butter on hot toast. And the needle made a pincushion of my finger with each loop of the thread. I longed for a shortcut, thinking, 'If only I could just staple the button back on!'

In this moment of frustration, I thought about how I have looked for shortcuts all of my life: I cheated in school tests to avoid endless study; I made myself 'happy' through drug and alcohol abuse; I 'did my time' in challenging relationships instead of nurturing them. Bible verses like Romans 5:3–5 helped me realise that what I had was a character problem; I was wishing that everything hard or time-consuming would just go away. As a result of Bible study and prayer, I now ask God to help me through challenges instead of finding shortcuts around them.

The Bible promises that good will result when we endure difficulties with patience. Perseverance will produce character. And character will produce hope. When Christians are known by perseverance, character and hope, we draw others to a life of serving Christ.

Prayer: *O God, help us to be patient as we go about our day, especially when we are frustrated and about to give up. Amen*

Thought for the day: Perseverance is handling difficult situations with godly character.

Avon White (Tennessee, US)

Plain Speech

Read Mark 1:16–20

Jesus said, 'Why do you call me "Lord, Lord", and do not do what I tell you? I will show you what someone is like who comes to me, hears my words, and acts on them.'

Luke 6:46–47 (NRSV)

I love language. I have studied foreign languages. I have studied prose and poetry, speeches and interviews. One thing I have learned is that language, no matter how beautiful or subtle, is useless if it does not clearly express meaning.

Jesus speaks plainly when he tells us to love one another, to do right by God and our neighbour, and to be kind and compassionate. But sometimes we want to debate the meaning of the word 'love', argue about all the ways in which 'right action' can be interpreted, or explain why some people are not 'worthy' of kindness.

I have learned the less talk the better. All that noise we make is really just the sound of us making excuses. 'No, Lord, I'm not ready to do that.' 'No, Lord, it's too much to ask.' 'No, Lord, I have a few things I want to do first. Just give me some time.'

When Jesus called the disciples, they did not make excuses. They followed. Plain speech demands a clear response. And the Lord does call us—all the time. God is not inviting a discussion; he is merely awaiting our response.

Prayer: *Dear Lord, help us to reflect your love in plain speech and compassionate actions, that we may be your worthy disciples. Amen*

Thought for the day: Let our words be clear to express God's love.

Barbara D. Price (Pennsylvania, US)

Make Me a Blessing

Read Matthew 25:32–40

The one who is in you is greater than the one who is in the world.
1 John 4:4 (NRSV)

When I was a child, my pastor and his wife made a real difference in my life. One year they even took me on holiday with them. They and other special people have truly been a blessing to me. Their gentleness, thoughtfulness, kindness and uplifting spirits have inspired me to become a means for God to bless others.

As I have grown older, I have found that being preoccupied with my own problems—physical infirmities, financial troubles or difficult relationships—can keep me from seeing the needs of others and stand in the way of my helping them.

The solution lies in remembering that our God is greater than our problems. Knowing that God will take care of us enables us to shift our focus away from ourselves toward helping others. Only when we let go of self-centredness and become truly concerned about another's welfare can we then act to meet that person's needs.

Prayer: *All-powerful God, give us opportunities to show your love by caring for others. In Christ's name. Amen*

Thought for the day: Despite my weaknesses and struggles, God can work through me to bless others.

David Ted De Hass (Iowa, US)

God's Awesome Care

Read Psalm 29:1–11

The Lord is close to the brokenhearted and saves those who are crushed in spirit.
Psalm 34:18 (NIV)

Ever since I was a small child I've enjoyed the fun, beauty and tranquillity of the beach. Now in my 60s, I have taken up a new hobby of collecting broken pieces of old glass that have been tumbled and smoothed by the sea and sand and washed up on shore.

Recently, as I found pieces of glass along the beach, I began to think about the similarity between this beautiful glass and our lives. We experience brokenness caused by painful or sorrowful situations. Just as the broken pieces of glass are made beautiful again by the waves of the sea, rocks and sand, we can be made whole, right, good and beautiful through God's tender love and care. I Peter 5:7 tells us, 'Cast all your anxiety on him because he cares for you.' We can give to God our broken lives, knowing that he will make us new.

Prayer: *Almighty and loving God, creator of heaven and earth, thank you for loving us and making us new. May we be aware of your loving care in all the situations of our lives as we pray, 'Our Father in heaven, hallowed be your name, your kingdom come, your will be done, on earth as it is in heaven. Give us today our daily bread. And forgive us our debts, as we also have forgiven our debtors. And lead us not into temptation, but deliver us from the evil one.'* Amen*

Thought for the day: God's care for us, like ocean waves, is never-ending.

Marsha Raye Smith (Virginia, US)

* Matthew 6:9–13 (NIV)

Reaching Toward Christ

Read Luke 6:12–19
All in the crowd were trying to touch him, for power came out from him and healed all of them.
Luke 6:19 (NRSV)

When I come to church, I immediately begin to search for God. As the scriptures are read and preached, I listen for what God will say to me. He always has a word for me. I love singing for Jesus and spending time in his presence.

Sometimes I struggle to get past the thoughts, anxieties and busyness in my mind and soul. Worship allows me to reconnect with my faith and be immersed in Christ's presence. It's almost as though I can touch him. I am healed from hurt, anxiety, fatigue and hopelessness. I love life again. I love people.

Through worship we can be renewed and inspired to serve Christ and proclaim the good news. We have a place, the church, and we have a time, during worship, when we can reach out to the Lord and be filled anew with faith, hope and love.

Prayer: *Dear Lord, thank you for always having a word to encourage us, time to be with us and power to heal us. Amen*

Thought for the day: What is preventing me from meeting with the Lord today?

Tatiana Menshova (Hrodna, Belarus)

Hiding from God

Read Jonah 1:3–17; 2:10
*'Who can hide in secret places so that I cannot see them?' declares the
Lord.*
Jeremiah 23:24 (NIV)

When I wake up my daughter in the morning, she pulls the covers
over her head in an attempt to hide from me. In some ways this is
an extension of a game we played when she was very little. In the
game she would cover herself up, and I would pretend that she had
disappeared. Then I would act surprised when she appeared from
under the covers. It was a fun game, but of course I knew where she
was the whole time.

Our attempts to hide from God are similar; he always knows where
to find us. The Bible is filled with stories of people who thought they
could hide from God: Adam and Eve hid in the Garden of Eden after
they had eaten the forbidden fruit; Jonah hid from God when he fled
to Tarshish after God told him to go to Nineveh; in secret, Judas
made his agreement with the temple leaders to betray Jesus, thinking no one saw his treachery. The fact is that we can never hide from
God, who is aware of all our comings and goings.

God's omniscience is a comfort as we encounter a world filled
with danger and the unknown. How wonderful it is to know that
wherever we are and whenever we pray, our loving Parent sees us
and knows us!

Prayer: *Dear God, help us always to be comforted with the knowledge
that we never need try to hide from you and that your presence is life
itself. Amen*

Thought for the day: Am I hiding from God or comforted by his
presence?

Matthew Reger (Ohio, US)

Giving Way to Others

Read 1 Corinthians 13:4–7
Do nothing out of selfish ambition or vain conceit. Rather, in humility value others above yourselves, not looking to your own interests but each of you to the interests of the others.
Philippians 2:3–4 (NIV)

Every time I leave my rural home, I have to drive a few miles down a very narrow road. I have to go slowly around blind bends to avoid a collision with oncoming cars. When two cars meet, one car has to pull over to let the other one pass. And if the road is particularly narrow with nowhere to pull over, one car must back up to a passing place so that both can proceed.

This back-road driving reminds me of what it means to 'love your neighbour as yourself' (Matthew 19:19). Such love means being considerate to others, making their way easier and thinking about their welfare before my own. Sometimes, it means I must give up something or delay my own needs to help another.

What a blessing it is to be open to the needs of others who might be in a tight spot and to find 'wide spaces' to help them move forward in their journey! We too are blessed when we receive the gifts others give to help us on our way.

Prayer: *Dear God, give us a sense of the needs of others and a willingness to serve them in whatever way we can. Amen*

Thought for the day: Jesus showed us how to put the needs of others above our own.

Mary Quick (West Virginia, US)

In Jesus' Name

Read Matthew 26:36–44

Jesus said, 'You may ask me for anything in my name, and I will do it.'
John 14:14 (NIV)

When I read Jesus' words, 'I will do whatever you ask in my name' (John 14:13), I realise that—in a sense—God's power is at my disposal. So, I reason, this means that I can force goodness and get revenge on those who don't live up to my standards! But wait. My will should match God's will. I have to ask in Jesus' name—with Jesus' purpose and motives. I cannot act out of indignation or inflict my self-righteous judgements upon others. Instead, invoking God's power means redeeming damaged souls and advancing loving relationships—motives that reflect God's will for the world.

Jesus struggled in Gethsemane to bring his will into alignment with God's will. Jesus' request, 'Let this cup pass from me' (Matthew 26:39, NRSV), did not stop there. Jesus added, '… yet not what I want but what you want'. Sometimes my prayers become an intense wrestling match to bring my will under God's will so that I can pray effectively for the person or event that concerns me. Praying in Jesus' name helps us to see those we're praying for through God's eyes and to love them with his love. Then, as God addresses our needs within the concerns we express, he can bring some healing to our lives as well.

Prayer: *Dear Lord, help us to trust that your will is always the most loving and merciful way. Amen*

Thought for the day: When I struggle to follow God's will, I know that he will bring about the best possible outcome.

George Nye (Oregon, US)

No Earning Required

Read Ephesians 2:1–10

'I know the plans I have for you,' declares the Lord, 'plans to prosper you and not to harm you, plans to give you hope and a future.'
Jeremiah 29:11 (NIV)

For seven years during my 20s, I struggled with an eating disorder. Today, despite many full and rewarding years of recovery from this vicious disease, I still struggle with self-esteem issues. I am a mother, wife and nurse. I volunteer my time and pledge my financial resources. I commit to a daily quiet time and strive to be an example to others. I was brought up in a strong Christian home, and I know that we are saved by grace, and not through any works. Yet despite all I have learned of God's grace, I confess that sometimes deep down I still feel I have to earn that grace.

Just as Paul had his 'thorn in the flesh', I have my 'thorn in the mind'. Twenty-seven years ago God granted me 'surrender' with my eating disorder, helping me to have a healthy attitude toward food and perfectionism. Now God continues to grant me daily surrender in my mind. He is love, even love for me just as I am.

Prayer: *Dear heavenly Father, thank you for saving us and for loving us, even when we find it hard to love ourselves. Use us as witnesses to your grace and mercy. Amen*

Thought for the day: God's grace is freely given.

Janice Quinn (Texas, US)

From Disorder to Peace

Read 1 Corinthians 1:8–13

God is not a God of disorder but of peace.
1 Corinthians 14:33 (NIV)

Two-year-old Alex stood in the middle of a pile of toys and colouring books that he had just thrown to the floor. Earlier, he had hit another two-year-old boy. As one of the volunteers who work with toddlers in our church crèche, I regularly encounter moments of chaos. This time, for the sake of the other children, I knew that I needed to restore order as quickly as possible. I decided to sit on the floor and talk with Alex. After he had calmed down, I explained why hitting other children and throwing toys were not good choices. When we had finished talking, Alex decided to help me pick up the toys and books. With a little encouragement, he also walked over to the boy he had hit and gave him a hug.

We all encounter days when our communities seem chaotic and divided, but today's reading tells us that ours is not a God of disorder. Instead, God wants us to enjoy lives filled with order, peace and love. When we accept God's standard and conduct ourselves in fitting and orderly ways—whether in worship, in our jobs or at home—we honour God and reflect his character.

Prayer: *Dear Lord, help us to conduct ourselves in ways that draw people to you. Amen*

Thought for the day: God can give us peace in any situation.

James C. Hendrix (Indiana, US)

Taking the Time

Read Psalm 40:1–10

Many, Lord my God, are the wonders you have done, the things you planned for us.
Psalm 40:5 (NIV)

Recently the harsh weather made it impossible for me to continue my outdoor activities, so I took a rare turn on our treadmill. While exercising, I listened to classical music. One of the pieces, 'The Minute Waltz', a lively number with a quick tempo, motivated me to go faster. For a few minutes I managed it, but my body resisted this added demand. I had to slow down to a pace I could handle.

Similarly, we sometimes jump into or accept new challenges that crowd our schedules and our lives. The result is that we are not efficient or fulfilled in any endeavour.

God tells Jeremiah, 'I know the plans I have for you... plans to prosper you and not to harm you, plans to give you hope and a future' (Jeremiah 29:11). But I often wonder how we can know God's plans for us. By taking time to read and meditate on God's word in scripture and spending time with him in prayer, we can learn to trust him. For me, the first line of a beloved hymn is a helpful reminder of how to grow closer to God: 'Take time to be holy, speak oft with thy Lord' (William D. Longstaff, c.1882).

Prayer: *Dear faithful God, forgive us when we fail to include you in our daily walk. We want to know your will and to follow you wherever you want us to go. Amen*

Thought for the day: God knows what we need; are we listening?

Walter N. Maris (Missouri, US)

My Daughter's Wedding

Read Isaiah 55:8–13

My thoughts are not your thoughts, nor are your ways my ways, says the Lord.
Isaiah 55:8 (NRSV)

Arranged marriages are still common in India. When it was time for my daughter to marry she left the decision to her family to find a suitable match for her. We asked our friends and church members to look for a groom for her. For three long years we scrutinised a number of potential grooms, but failed to find the right person. We were overcome with frustration and disappointment.

Despite our difficulties we continued to pray with friends and church members for a suitable match. Then Daniel came along and everything fell into place. Soon my daughter and Daniel were married, and our hearts were filled with joy.

Later, when I was reading from Isaiah, I realised that God's ways and his plans are often different from ours. When things do not go our way at the time we expect, we can fail to see God's purpose. But he knows what is right for us.

Prayer: *Thank you, God, for all your tender mercies. We are ever grateful and indebted to you and we praise your holy name. Amen*

Thought for the day: I will wait upon the Lord, who knows my every need.

G. Selva Kumar (Karnataka, India)

Learning to Walk

Read Philippians 1:6–7, 2:13

Who are you to judge someone else's servants? They stand or fall before their own Lord (and they will stand, because the Lord has the power to make them stand).
Romans 14:4 (CEB)

When children learn to walk, falling is an expected part of the process. In the same way, adults learning something new should not expect to succeed immediately. As we are growing in spiritual maturity, failures will come. Failing makes us human.

We are imperfect, unfinished works in progress. Even the apostle Paul admitted, 'It's not that I have already reached [the] goal [of being conformed to Christ's death] or have already been perfected, but I pursue it, so that I may grab hold of it because Christ grabbed hold of me for just this purpose' (Philippians 3:12). Striving to grow and change—to become spiritually mature—is a never-ending process.

Just as falling does not startle small children—or their parents—God is not surprised when we stumble or fall. Instead, he assures us that we are forgiven. For when we stumble into sin, we also find God's grace.

Prayer: *Dear Father, thank you for helping us as we stumble our way through becoming spiritually mature. Amen*

Thought for the day: Whether walking or stumbling, we are God's children.

Jeff Adams (Arizona, US)

On Trees and Fruits

Read Psalm 1:1–6

Jesus said, 'This is to my Father's glory, that you bear much fruit, showing yourselves to be my disciples.'
John 15:8 (NIV)

Today I decided to prune two trees in my garden. One of them was small, the other much larger. The small one was a challenge, since I had to lower myself to cut down the dry branches. But the work was minimal compared to the task of cutting the higher and more robust branches of the larger tree.

While working, I thought about how God cares for us. In the fallow seasons of our lives, God is the gardener who assesses our branches, removes everything that may prevent us from producing fruit in the next season, and prepares us for the new season to come. However, the process of change can be painful.

The reward for the hard work of pruning comes with the first drops of rain that fall in the spring. Strengthened, the trees in my garden can focus their energies on new green branches. Life is renewed. Likewise, we can be strengthened by the changes God makes during our fallow seasons. He cares for us. He knows exactly what to remove and what to preserve so that we will bear fruit in the coming seasons.

Prayer: *Dear God, thank you for pruning us so that we can bear good fruit in all stages of our lives. Amen*

Thought for the day: God sees my potential for beauty and fruitfulness.

Samara L. Martins D'Armada Matos (Minas Gerais, Brazil)

Looking Forward

Read Philippians 3:10–14

I forget about the things behind me and reach out for the things ahead of me. The goal I pursue is the prize of God's upward call in Christ Jesus.
Philippians 3:13–14 (CEB)

I volunteer with a ministry that helps ex-offenders to make the transition back into society. All of these men made mistakes, broke the law, and served time in prison. Many of them find it difficult to look beyond their past failures. I want them to realise that all of us have made mistakes. Most of us tend to look back at our failures with regret, anger, shame and sadness.

The Bible is full of stories about people who made serious mistakes. Moses was a murderer. David committed adultery. Peter abandoned Jesus on the night he was arrested. And Paul persecuted the followers of Christ. Rather than dwelling on their past mistakes, each of these men, through the grace of God, went on to do great things for the kingdom. Their stories provide inspiration for all of us to do the same.

We can learn from our past mistakes, but it is also important to look to the future. By accepting Christ as our Saviour, we can experience forgiveness and delight in a life of honouring and serving him.

Prayer: *Dear God, thank you for easing the pain of failure and making us free to serve you. Through Jesus Christ, we pray. Amen*

Thought for the day: All who accept Christ receive a fresh start.

John Bown (Minnesota, US)

Closed Gates

Read Hebrews 12:1–6

Faith is the reality of what we hope for, the proof of what we don't see.
Hebrews 11:1 (CEB)

We had planned a lovely walk along a footpath through the wooded hillsides. The signposts at the beginning of the footpath seemed crystal clear. Even so we took a wrong turn. When we finally got on to the right path we came up against a closed gate. Disappointed and resigned, we were about to turn back. But then we saw people coming toward us from beyond the gate. We had not noticed a very narrow path beside the gate that enabled us to skirt this obstacle and proceed without difficulty.

Reflecting on this later, I realised how our failure to notice the way forward is similar to the way I live my faith. Sometimes, facing what I think are insurmountable walls of problems and troubles, and too busy scrambling for a way out, I fail to see the solution that the Lord has already prepared for me. I have come to see that instead of allowing anxiety and discouragement to hold us back, we can trust God's ability to act in situations where we see no solution.

Prayer: *Dear Lord, thank you for being our way to safety in the face of all difficulties. Open our hearts and enable us to see beyond the 'closed gates' of our life. Amen*

Thought for the day: When the way seems impossible, God provides a path forward.

Elisa Boetti (Piedmont, Italy)

Sweet Dreams

Read Psalm 27:1–6

In the day of trouble [the Lord] will keep me safe in his dwelling; he will hide me in the shelter of his sacred tent and set me high upon a rock.
Psalm 27:5 (NIV)

At a time when I felt very lost and overwhelmed with anxiety, I had a dream that filled me with peace and hope. In this dream I was a small child again and all alone. A strong man was nearby repairing an old abandoned well. He lifted me up and set me on a high wall where I could watch him. I felt safe in his care. He told me to have a drink of fresh well water. He told me that it was the purest water I would ever taste.

The Bible tells stories about God's speaking to people in their dreams (see Genesis 37 and 40 and also Matthew 1 and 2). After many days of reflection, I became convinced that God had spoken to me in this strange, wonderful dream.

My dream helped me see that God loves me and will always take care of me. My deep depression has slowly lifted from my mind and heart as each day I trust my heavenly Father. I know that God will continue to lift me up, set me on a high safe wall, and refresh me with living water.

Prayer: *Ever-loving God, thank you for the gift of restful, restorative sleep. Amen*

Thought for the day: I can trust God to nurture me.

Nancy J. Stauffer (Georgia, US)

PRAYER FOCUS: SOMEONE SUFFERING FROM INSOMNIA

The Power of Salt

Read 2 Corinthians 5:17–20

You are the salt of the earth.
Matthew 5:13 (NRSV)

Throughout history, salt has been highly valued. It is used to preserve food and enhance the flavour of food. Salt is also used to mix with water for cleaning and it is an ingredient in toothpaste to help clean and strengthen teeth.

On 17 January 2013, I learned of another use for salt. It was the morning of the dedication service for the new church building for Prachakittisuk Church at Mae Sai, Chiang Rai, Thailand. As part of the dedication ceremony, an ice sculptor had carved a beautiful cross. Just as he finished the carving, one side of the cross broke off. The sculptor quickly put salt around the cracked area and then linked the broken part back to its original position. After he had held it firmly for a few minutes, the two parts were solidly reconnected.

That event led me to think about our mission from Jesus: to be the salt of the earth. He wants us to be the connecting and reconciling power among people who are broken, who have forgotten or have never known the love of God. It's the mission that Paul wrote of in 2 Corinthians: 'God was reconciling the world to himself in Christ... And he has committed to us the message of reconciliation.'

Prayer: *O God, by your grace we commit ourselves to be the salt of the earth, to help bring together your family into one community under your love and care. Amen*

Thought for the day: Through the power of Christ, I can help reconcile others to God.

Somnuek Jaripen (Chiang Mai, Thailand)

Come and See

Read John 4:7–42

The Samaritan woman said to the people of the town, 'Come, see a man who told me everything I ever did. Could this be the Messiah?'
John 4:29 (NIV)

My life seems bland. I wonder who would want to follow Christ because of me. Still, I pray for courage and ask God to give me words that others need to hear.

When a friend noticed that I read my Bible during my break, she asked, 'Is this what keeps you calm?' We talked about my daily devotions. As a result, she has resolved to start her own practice of prayer and Bible study.

Not long afterward, a relative asked me to pray with her regarding her troubled marriage. Now we pray every day. Sometimes I come across a passage of scripture for her to read. I talk about my struggles with worry and fear and tell her how God's word gives me peace. I have realised that I am witnessing to the hope I find in Jesus and it's encouraging to her.

I am struck by the simplicity of the woman's invitation in John 4:29: 'Come, see.' Her words led many people to believe in Jesus. When we are open, our lives naturally reflect the transforming love and power of Christ. Even if our lives seem bland, others notice our joy and peace and want to understand. The only invitation we need to extend is this: 'Come, see.' The Holy Spirit will do the rest.

Prayer: *Heavenly Lord, help us share your message of redemption and love. Amen*

Thought for the day: Someone who needs to hear about Jesus is close by.

Dorothea M. Love (California, US)

PRAYER FOCUS: SOMEONE WHO WITNESSES BY QUIET EXAMPLE

Puzzled by Life?

Read Deuteronomy 10:12–13
Your word is a lamp for my feet, a light on my path.'
Psalm 119:105 (NIV)

I enjoy doing jigsaw puzzles, but I rely on the puzzle maker to guide me. Once I worked on a puzzle in which written clues, instead of a picture on the box, described the finished puzzle. I worked out what objects were in the puzzle, but I couldn't determine their colour or where they were supposed to be in relation to one another. Without a picture, I didn't have the guidance I needed to put the puzzle together.

In a similar way, we need our Maker to provide guidance for our lives. God's guidance is found throughout the Bible, but for me is summed up in the ten commandments (Exodus 20:1–17) and the Sermon on the Mount (Matthew 5—7).

Failing to follow God's guidance leads to poor decisions and destructive behaviour. Proverbs 14:12 points out that 'there is a way that appears to be right, but in the end it leads to death'. On the other hand, those who follow God's guidance are described as 'a tree planted by streams of water, which yields its fruit in season… whatever they do prospers' (Psalm 1:3). We can make better sense of the puzzle of our lives when we study the Bible and obey God's commands.

Prayer: *Dear God, when we are puzzled about how to live, lead us to the guidance you have provided in your word. Amen*

Thought for the day: The Bible is our guidebook for living.

David B. Smith (Oregon, US)

A Much Loved Baby

Read Romans 8:35–39

The Lord appeared to us in the past, saying: 'I have loved you with an everlasting love; I have drawn you with unfailing kindness.'
Jeremiah 31:3 (NIV)

Jason lay snug in his mother's arms, sometimes cooing and sometimes crying. Doting aunts and uncles tickled his cheek and stroked his tiny outstretched fingers. The relatives resorted to the usual baby talk, which was unintelligible to everyone, including the baby. But whatever was said or cooed, one thing was obvious; the baby was completely loved and adored.

Jason had done nothing to deserve the love that his family lavished on him. He hadn't been clever, gained a degree or helped the poor. Their love was unconditional. They loved him just for who he was; he didn't have to do anything.

God has that kind of love for us. We cannot do anything to deserve his love. He has loved us from before the beginning of time and will continue to love us for all eternity. No good works, sacrifice or deprivation can earn that love. All we can do is accept God's love and redemption.

Prayer: *Thank you, heavenly Father, that we do not have to earn your love. As Jesus taught us, we pray, 'Father, hallowed be your name, your kingdom come. Give us each day our daily bread. Forgive us our sins, for we also forgive everyone who sins against us. And lead us not into temptation.'* Amen

Thought for the day: God's love for us is even greater than an earthly parent's love.

Carol Purves (Cumbria, England)

PRAYER FOCUS: PARENTS OF NEW BABIES   129
* Luke 11:2–4 (NIV)

Green Pastures

Read Isaiah 41:17–20

The Lord said, 'I will make rivers flow on barren heights, and springs within the valleys. I will turn the desert into pools of water, and the parched ground into springs.'

Isaiah 41:18 (NIV)

South Texas was suffering from drought. For the entire summer, we had received only a few inches of rain. The temperature reached 100 degrees or higher 20 days in a row. Fields were barren. Farmers were forced to sell livestock because they had no grass.

Lack of rainwater is only one kind of drought that may invade our lives. Others can be a divorce, illness or the loss of a loved one, job or home. Our souls may be parched from lack of nourishment. During those times, we can trust that God will send showers of blessing. We Texans have a saying, 'It always rains at the end of a dry spell!' We know that a drought, although difficult, is temporary. In the same way, we Christians can know that after a dry spell, we simply have to trust God and be patient and we will see the rain again.

Prayer: *Dear God, help us to trust you and wait patiently for your blessings. Amen*

Thought for the day: When my soul is parched, God can sustain me.

Lu Fullilove (Texas, US)

Faith and Healing

Read Matthew 9:18–26

As [Jesus] went along, he saw a man blind from birth. His disciples asked him, 'Rabbi, who sinned, this man or his parents, that he was born blind?'
John 9:1–2 (NIV)

As a doctor I am blessed to see God's healing every day. Seeing an injured or ill person find healing is a powerful experience and one that strengthens my faith in God. People of faith often show extraordinary trust in God's presence with them when illness befalls them or a loved one. I believe their faith plays a role in the healing process.

But what about those individuals and families who have great faith but are not healed? Is something in their faith lacking? Are they being punished for some grievous sin? Our scripture verse from the Gospel of John suggests that Jesus' disciples thought so. But I don't believe our loving God acts in that way. His love for us is unfailing. He feels our suffering. And we can have hope that '[God] will wipe every tear from [our] eyes. There will be no more death or mourning or crying or pain, for the old order of things has passed away' (Revelation 21:4).

I have learned that while healing is certainly a gift from God, the absence of physical healing does not indicate the absence of God or a lack of faith on the part of his beloved children. No matter what the outcome is, God walks with us and strengthens us.

Prayer: *Dear God, thank you for always being with us, even in the darkest of times. In Jesus' name we pray. Amen*

Thought for the day: God has promised never to leave us or forsake us.

Mark Karpinski (North Carolina, US)

PRAYER FOCUS: DOCTORS

Stopping to Listen

Read Psalm 32:1–11

Be still, and know that I am God! I am exalted among the nations, I am exalted in the earth.
Psalm 46:10 (NRSV)

I have a friend who speaks slowly, pausing before she answers a question, or even in the middle of a sentence. She stops to chuckle when she's retelling a funny story. Sometimes when listening to her I have felt impatient, wanting to jump in and finish a sentence for her. But I dislike it when people do that to me, which reminds me not to treat her in that way either. I just have to remember when we're talking to relax and let her say things in her own way.

I have realised that slowing down to listen is a good habit for me in my prayer time, too. I tend to tell God my concerns and requests at high speed before running off to the rest of my day. I know God wants to hear all these things from me, and I can't think faster than he can listen. But I don't hear very well while I'm thinking; so unless I quiet my brain during some of my time with God, I probably won't hear all the things he wants to tell me. Since I have the assurance that God wants to teach and counsel me, the least I can do is take time to listen.

Prayer: *Forgive us, Lord, for letting our speaking and listening get out of balance during our time with you. Thank you for your patience and your love that never ends. Amen*

Thought for the day: Do I listen to God the way he listens to me?

Jennifer Aaron (Washington, US)

Small Group Questions

Wednesday 6 May

1. Have you had an experience similar to the one Phyllis describes? How did you feel when you had not heard from your loved one in a long time? What did you do? How did you respond when they finally contacted you?

2. When have you felt separated from God? How did you listen for God's voice during that time? What prayers or spiritual practices helped you to reconnect to him and to your faith?

3. For this writer, how could 'No news is good news' help? How might this be an answer or response to her prayers?

4. How do you think the parable of the prodigal son and this writer's circumstances compare? How do they differ?

5. Do you talk with God every day or only when you're experiencing stress? What is the value of 'talking with God every day'?

6. Phyllis states 'that time of not knowing deepened my faith in God'. Is that the way you would have reacted in this situation? Why or why not?

7. How do you define what 'pray without ceasing' means? How do you do this?

Wednesday 13 May

1. Who has been your 'Barnabas'? Describe this person. How does this person encourage you? How does this person's example help you to encourage others?

2. Derl suggests that 'we can come alongside [others] and simply be present with them' in times of tragedy and struggle. Recall a time when someone did this for you. How did that person's presence help you through a difficult time?

3. If someone who was hurting came to you, would you be more likely to listen with criticism and judgement or with compassion? Do you think that some circumstances call for judgement or is compassion always the proper response? Why or why not?

4. Which Bible verses would you recommend to console someone and lift their spirits? How do you think Barnabas might have encouraged others during his ministry 2000 years ago?

5. Do you find it easy to encourage others? Whom and how do you encourage?

6. In what way was your mother or father an example for you to follow?

Wednesday 20 May

1. Read Romans 5:1–11. What do you think Paul means when he writes, 'we boast in the hope of God's glory' and 'we even take pride in God through our Lord Jesus Christ'? How do you personally relate to these statements?

2. Recall a time when you were so proud of something (an achievement, a relationship, etc.) that you told a stranger about it. How did it feel to share your pride with another person? How did that person react?

3. What are the two most important relationships in your life? Why are these relationships important to you? What is each relationship based on—love, need, respect, gratitude or something else?

4. Which Bible verse best expresses for you the relationship God has with you? How does this verse offer assurance to you?

5. What were you most proud of growing up? Why?

6. What element of your identity are you most willing to communicate to others? Why?

Wednesday 27 May

1. Do you appreciate or resent kind criticism from your friends and family? Describe a time when you found someone's criticism to be helpful. Why was it helpful? How did the person share the criticism with you? Did the manner in which the criticism was shared affect the way you received it?

2. How does your church community admonish inappropriate behaviour or word choice? Do you find this practice helpful or harmful? How might your church help people to think about the way their words and actions shape and reflect their relationship with God?

3. Do you admire or disdain Sherry's gentle/tender admonishment of Ginger's choice of expression (words)? When do you think it's not appropriate to challenge someone's choice of words?

4. Besides exclamations like 'O my god!' or 'Oh god!' that we frequently hear in our everyday vernacular, can you think of some other ways we sometimes take God's name in vain? How might a 'habit of speech' like this affect one's relationship with God?

5. How are we sometimes too 'careless or blind to see' habits and behaviour that could be an affront to God or others around us?

6. What was the biggest change you had to make when you became a Christian? What helped you in your struggle with the ungodly habits of your previous life?

7. Would you have responded to a friend's rebuke in the same way that Ginger did? Why or why not?

8. When have you been rebuked by a Christian friend? When have you been the one rebuking?

Wednesday 3 June

1. What do you think Susan means by 'listening to our bodies'? Is it easy or hard for you to pay attention to the needs and limits of your body? What spiritual practices or exercises help you to listen to your body?

2. 1 Corinthians 6:19 states, 'Don't you know that your body is a temple of the Holy Spirit who is in you?' (CEB). How do you care for your body? What does it mean to you to treat your body as a temple of the Holy Spirit?

3. How could stress and fatigue affect our faith? Do you think of rest as a 'choice' or a 'requirement' for yourself?

4. Where do you 'draw the line' to avoid exhaustion when pushing yourself to complete a task or achieve a goal? What are some warning signs when we've pushed ourselves too far?

5. What does the Bible say about work and rest? From a biblical perspective, which do you think is more significant? Why?

6. How easy is it for you to rest? Why do you think it's hard for some people to relax and rest?

7. How difficult is it for you to hand over your worries to God? What has made it easier for you?

Wednesday 10 June

1. How do you prefer to read and study the Bible? Alone? With a group? Only in worship on Sundays? Why is this your preference?

2. How does reading the Bible help you to better 'live as part of God's family in the world'? What does it mean to you to be a member of God's family? How does being a member of the family of God affect the way you interact with other people?

3. How would you respond to someone who asks you, 'Who are you? Where do you come from?' How would your reply differ if you answered these questions from a spiritual perspective?

4. Through whom did you learn most about your extended family? What gives you pride or humility about your family from what you've heard over time?

5. What do you know about our biblical 'ancestors in the faith' that makes you proud today? What is/will be your part in the story of God's family?

6. Who have been your faith mentors?

7. What person or situation do you most relate to in the scriptures? Why?

Wednesday 17 June

1. How do you and your family acknowledge important life events? Do you recognise important events in your faith in the same way? Why or why not?

2. What experiences or events does your church recognise as important or significant? What do you like about the way your church celebrates baptisms, Communion, confirmation or weddings? How do these events shape the community's life of faith?

3. For you personally, what is the most important part of your Christian experience up to now? Why is this so?

4. What assures you that you are undeniably 'a child of God'? Do you believe all people are 'children of God' or that only some people are? What does the Bible say that supports your belief?

5. Do you think someone could be a 'child of God' and later lose that status? Do you believe that our faith or God's grace makes us 'children of God' or is it something else? Why do you believe this?

6. Recount the day of your baptism and what it means to you.

7. Do you or your family do anything to commemorate one another's baptisms? If so, what? If not, why not?

Wednesday 24 June

1. When you hear the words 'thinking backwards' what comes to mind? How would you describe 'thinking backwards' to someone unfamiliar with the term? Is your association with thinking backwards positive or negative?

2. 2 Corinthians 4:18 tells us that 'what is seen is temporary, but what is unseen is eternal' (NIV). Is this a comforting statement to you? Why or why not? How does this verse affect the way you live your life?

3. What lessons about wealth and possessions can we learn from verses such as Matthew 6:24–33, Mark 10:17–31 and Luke 12:13–21? Do you think God is more concerned about our gathering wealth/possessions or our attitude regarding wealth/possessions? Which of these two categories is more evident in your life? Why?

4. How does your community of faith use its members' offerings to glorify God? What more could/should your church be doing 'to offer hospitality to others, provide for others' needs and act with compassion when we have the opportunity'?

5. Besides materialism, what do you see as backwards thinking in the society in which you live?

6. What have you done to resist backwards thinking and restore God's thinking within yourself and your sphere of influence?

Wednesday 1 July

1. Have you ever had an experience, like the one Margaret describes, where a stranger recognised you as a Christian? If so, was the experience positive or negative? How did they recognise your faith?

2. How do you recognise other Christians? Is it important to you to know whether or not someone is a Christian? Why or why not?

3. Margaret says she would rather people recognise her faith by her actions and conduct. What actions or habits do you try to incorporate in your life as you live out your faith?

4. Think of a person who has shown God's love to you. How did this person act or speak? What actions or practices did this person model that helped you to see God's love?

5. Which passages of scripture, spiritual practices or prayers help you to live out the teachings of Christ in your life?

Wednesday 8 July

1. In today's meditation, Andrew writes, 'there are no unimportant prayers'. Do you agree or disagree? Explain.

2. How do you prefer to pray? Alone? With a group? Using a written prayer? Saying what comes to your mind? Why do you prefer this form of prayer?

3. Describe a time when you felt very connected to God during prayer. Is this a frequent experience for you? If not, how do you feel about prayer?

4. Acts 1:14 states that members of the early church were 'constantly devoting themselves to prayer' (NRSV). How does your church community support or encourage prayer? What ministries, groups or practices does your church provide to help people strengthen their prayer lives?

5. Jesus stated, 'When you are praying, do not heap up empty phrases as the Gentiles do; for they think that they will be heard because of their many words' (Matthew 6:7, NRSV). What do you think he meant by 'empty phrases'? Do you think his admonition applies to private prayers or just public ones?

Wednesday 15 July

1. What family activities or outings do you remember from your childhood or from the early years of your children's lives?

2. Recall a time when you experienced a 'dead end' in your life. How did you feel at that time? To whom did you turn for help? How did this 'dead end' experience affect your faith?

3. When you are faced with an important decision, what do you do? Is there a particular person whose advice or counsel you seek?

4. How does your faith affect the way you approach decision-making? Are there scripture passages or prayers that are useful to you in your discernment process?

5. How does your church make decisions? Does this model seem to work well? What do you appreciate about your church's decision-making process? How do you think it might be improved?

Wednesday 22 July

1. Patricia writes, 'Loving those who love us is easy.' Do you agree or disagree with this statement? When have you found it difficult to love someone who loves you? How did you deal with this situation?

2. Do you think praying daily for someone who has hurt you is a way of 'laying down your life' for that person? If so, have you done this? If not, why not?

3. Read John 13:34–35. Who do you think Jesus is referring to when he says, 'love one another'?

4. Think of someone you find difficult to love. How will you pray for that person today? How will you pray for yourself as you seek to love that person better?

5. How does your church or community show hospitality and compassion to those whom society finds hard to love? What ministries or practices seek to show compassion and love to those in need or those who are often rejected?

Wednesday 29 July

1. What do you think of Delores' method for memorising and meditating on scripture? Would this method of focusing on only one part of a verse at a time be helpful to you?

2. Which scripture verses or passages have you memorised? Where did you learn them? Did you intentionally try to memorise them? Is memorising scripture a helpful spiritual discipline for you?

3. When you find yourself thinking negative thoughts or having a negative attitude, what do you do to change your thinking or behaviour?

4. How does your church encourage you and others to focus on whatever is true, noble, right, pure, lovely and admirable? Are there parts of your worship or particular songs or prayers that help you remember to focus on these things?

5. How does studying scripture shape or change your perspective? Think about a time when a scripture passage changed the way you thought about or responded to someone or something.

Wednesday 5 August

1. What was your initial reaction to Pavel's story? What parts of this story could you relate to personally?

2. For Pavel, this experience is an example of what Jesus meant when he said, 'unless you change and become like children, you will never enter the kingdom of heaven' (Matthew 18:3, NRSV). Do you agree or disagree?

3. What experiences have you had that help you understand this statement from Jesus? What do you think it means to 'become like children'? What actions, behaviour or attitudes should we adopt to 'become like children'?

4. When have you given selflessly or been the recipient of someone's sacrificial giving? How did this experience make you feel? How did the people in this situation respond? How did this experience affect your faith?

5. How does your church or community support single parents and people without proper housing? How can you become more involved in ministries that help people in situations like the one Pavel and David experienced?

Wednesday 12 August

1. What is your typical experience during worship? Is it a time of renewal and connection to God? Is it something you do out of habit? Is it a time of fellowship with others?

2. What distractions or worries prevent you from being fully attentive in worship? How do you deal with these distractions?

3. Do you worship for God's sake, for your own or for some combination of the two?

4. How does your church or community understand the purpose of worship? Why does your church gather to worship? What rituals, activities or prayers take place only during worship?

5. Other than worship in a church, where do you feel most connected to God? Where do you go when you need to be renewed and inspired to love and serve him?

Wednesday 19 August

1. What surprised you about Selva's story? What parts of this story sounded familiar or were similar to your own experience or that of someone you know?

2. Describe a time when you prayed and hoped for something to happen, and it seemed that God was silent. How did you feel during that time? How did your prayers change as you waited for God's answer?

3. Selva says that despite disappointment and frustration, they continued to pray. Do you find it easy or difficult to continue to pray when you are frustrated or disappointed? What helps you to persevere in prayer?

4. What scripture passages do you find comforting or helpful in times of waiting?

5. Selva's community supported them through prayer during this experience. How has your church community supported you during difficult times? Was it meaningful to you that others were praying for you and for your situation?

Wednesday 26 August

1. Have you ever felt like Dorothea, that your life of faith was bland? What made you feel this way? In what way did you wish your life to be different?

2. How do you think a Christian life should look or be lived? Describe someone who is a strong witness for Christ.

3. What friendships have you formed because of a shared faith? Where did you meet these people and how did you become friends? How do these friendships support or encourage you in your faith?

4. What activities or mission opportunities does your church offer? Who could you invite to 'come, see' your faith community in action?

5. Have you ever been invited to visit a friend's church or faith community? Did you accept the invitation? Describe your experience.

I Think It's God Calling

A vocation diary

Katy Magdalene Price

All Katy Magdalene really wanted was an easy life, but something was nagging away at her. Eventually, both she and her husband realised what that something was: a vocation to ordained ministry, the very last thing that either of them expected. But God was calling—and God is nothing if not patient, as she discovered. And then everything changed...

This is a lively personal account of one young woman's journey from atheist to curate in the Anglican Church. She shares the emotional and spiritual ups and downs of theological training, personal formation and finally ordination itself, as well as the challenges for family and friends from such a major change of direction.

ISBN 978 1 84101 645 0   £7.99

To order a copy of this book, please turn to the order form on page 159.

The Twelve Degrees of Silence

Marie-Aimée de Jésus OCD
Edited by Lucinda M. Vardey

The stresses and strains of contemporary life leave so many of us thirsting for peace and clarity of mind and heart. While we may sense that constant distraction hinders spiritual growth, we find it hard to cultivate attitudes of peace and stillness. We may long to experience closer communion with God, yet feel overwhelmed by the many demands on our attention.

This book invites us to nurture a spirituality of silence through the words and wisdom of the 19th-century Carmelite and mystic, Sister Marie-Aimée de Jésus. Through a combination of her measured insights and exercises for personal application by author and spiritual teacher Lucinda M. Vardey, the reader is invited on a twelve-movement journey into a silent and intimate union with God. An introduction and biography of Marie-Aimée de Jésus explores her influence on other well-known Carmelites such as the saint and martyr Edith Stein.

ISBN 978 0 85746 407 1   £5.99
To order a copy of this book, please turn to the order form on page 159.

Help! It's the All-Age Slot

52 instant talk outlines for church services

Rebecca Parkinson

This resource offers material that is thoroughly enjoyable for adults and children alike. The talks are easy to use, all-age in presentation, and ensure that the theme will be communicated effectively.

- Covers key occasions in the church year plus more general themes
- Provides fresh material for a whole year
- Easy to adapt, with suggestions given

ISBN 978 0 85746 023 3   £9.99

To order a copy of this book, please turn to the order form on page 159.

Walking in their Shadow

Supporting children and young people through bereavement

Lex Bradley

How can you best support someone who is grieving?

This resource aims to equip children's and youth workers, church leaders and those working in a chaplaincy context to support bereaved children and young people.

Written with first-hand knowledge of the needs of both a bereaved young person and a concerned youth worker, Walking in their Shadow offers a unique combination of practical advice, biblical teaching and creative, therapeutic techniques to help the young person adjust to bereavement as a lifelong journey.

- Contains five session outlines themed around Holy Week.
- Each outline includes two age-differentiated stories, discussion starters, links to appropriate media clips, and creative, therapeutic activity ideas.
- Provides downloadable activity sheets and 'I need to tell you...' icebreaker cards.

ISBN 978 0 85746 255 8   £9.99
To order a copy of this book, please turn to the order form on page 159.

How to encourage Bible reading in your church

BRF has been helping individuals connect with the Bible for over 90 years. We want to support churches as they seek to encourage church members into regular Bible reading.

Order a Bible reading resources pack

This pack is designed to give your church the tools to publicise our Bible reading notes. It includes:

- Sample Bible reading notes for your congregation to try.
- Publicity resources, including a poster.
- A church magazine feature about Bible reading notes.

The pack is free, but we welcome a £5 donation to cover the cost of postage. If you require a pack to be sent outside the UK or require a specific number of sample Bible reading notes, please contact us for postage costs. More information about what the current pack contains is available on our website.

How to order and find out more
- Visit **www.biblereadingnotes.org.uk/for-churches/**
- Telephone BRF on 01865 319700 between 9.15 am and 5.30 pm.
- Write to us at BRF, 15 The Chambers, Vineyard, Abingdon, OX14 3FE.

Keep informed about our latest initiatives

We are continuing to develop resources to help churches encourage people into regular Bible reading, wherever they are on their journey. Join our email list at **www.biblereadingnotes.org.uk/helpingchurches/** to stay informed about the latest initiatives that your church could benefit from.

Introduce a friend to our notes

We can send information about our notes and current prices for you to pass on. Please contact us.

Subscriptions

The Upper Room is published in January, May and September.

Individual subscriptions

The subscription rate for orders for 4 or fewer copies includes postage and packing: THE UPPER ROOM annual individual subscription   £16.20

Church subscriptions

Orders for 5 copies or more, sent to ONE address, are post free:
THE UPPER ROOM annual church subscription   £12.75

Please do not send payment with order for a church subscription. We will send an invoice with your first order.

Please note that the annual billing period for church subscriptions runs from 1 May to 30 April.

Copies of the notes may also be obtained from Christian bookshops.

Single copies of *The Upper Room* will cost £4.25. Prices valid until 30 April 2016.

Giant print version

The Upper Room is available in giant print for the visually impaired, from:

Torch Trust for the Blind
Torch House
Torch Way,
Northampton Road
Market Harborough
LE16 9HL

Tel: 01858 438260
www.torchtrust.org

Individual Subscriptions

☐ I would like to take out a subscription myself (complete your name and address details only once)

☐ I would like to give a gift subscription (please complete both name and address sections below)

Your name...

Your address...

....Postcode...

Your telephone number...

Gift subscription name...

Gift subscription address..

....Postcode...

Gift message (20 words max)..

....

Please send *The Upper Room* beginning with the September 2015 / January 2016 / May 2016 issue: (delete as applicable)

THE UPPER ROOM ☐ £16.20

Please complete the payment details below and send, with appropriate payment, to: BRF, 15 The Chambers, Vineyard, Abingdon OX14 3FE

Total enclosed £ .... (cheques should be made payable to 'BRF')

Payment by ☐ cheque ☐ postal order ☐ Visa ☐ Mastercard ☐ Switch

Card no: ⬜⬜⬜⬜⬜⬜⬜⬜⬜⬜⬜⬜⬜⬜⬜⬜⬜⬜⬜⬜

Expires: ⬜⬜⬜⬜   Security code: ⬜⬜⬜

Issue no (Switch): ⬜⬜⬜⬜

Signature (essential if paying by credit/Switch card) ....

☐ Please do not send me further information about BRF publications

☐ Please send me a Bible reading resources pack to encourage Bible reading in my church

BRF is a Registered Charity

Church Subscriptions

☐ Please send me … copies of *The Upper Room* September 2015 / January 2016 / May 2016 issue (delete as applicable)

Name...

Address ....

....Postcode.................................

Telephone ....

Email..

Please send this completed form to:
BRF, 15 The Chambers, Vineyard, Abingdon OX14 3FE

Please do not send payment with this order. We will send an invoice with your first order.

Christian bookshops: All good Christian bookshops stock BRF publications. For your nearest stockist, please contact BRF.

Telephone: The BRF office is open between 09.15 and 17.30. To place your order, telephone 01865 319700; fax 01865 319701.

Web: Visit www.brf.org.uk

☐ Please send me a Bible reading resources pack to encourage Bible reading in my church

BRF is a Registered Charity

ORDERFORM

REF	TITLE	PRICE	QTY	TOTAL
645 0	I Think It's God Calling	£7.99		
407 1	The Twelve Degrees of Silence	£5.99		
023 3	Help! It's the All-Age Slot	£9.99		
255 8	Walking in their Shadow	£9.99		
		Postage and packing		
		Donation		
		TOTAL		

POSTAGE AND PACKING CHARGES				
Order value	UK	Europe	Economy (Surface)	Standard (Air)
Under £7.00	£1.25	£3.00	£3.50	£5.50
£7.00–£29.00	£2.25	£5.50	£6.50	£10.00
£30.00 and over	free	prices on request		

Name _____ Account Number _____

Address _____

_____ Postcode _____

Telephone Number_____

Email _____

Payment by: ❏ Cheque ❏ Mastercard ❏ Visa ❏ Postal Order ❏ Maestro

Card no ☐☐☐☐ ☐☐☐☐ ☐☐☐☐ ☐☐☐☐ ☐☐☐

Valid from ☐☐☐☐ Expires ☐☐☐☐ Issue no. ☐☐☐

Security code* ☐☐☐ *Last 3 digits on the reverse of the card. ESSENTIAL IN ORDER TO PROCESS YOUR ORDER Shaded boxes for Maestro use only

Signature _____ Date _____

All orders must be accompanied by the appropriate payment.

Please send your completed order form to:
BRF, 15 The Chambers, Vineyard, Abingdon OX14 3FE
Tel. 01865 319700 / Fax. 01865 319701 Email: enquiries@brf.org.uk

❏ Please send me further information about BRF publications.

Available from your local Christian bookshop.   BRF is a Registered Charity

About

BRF is a registered charity and also a limited company, and has been in existence since 1922. Through all that we do—producing resources, providing training, working face-to-face with adults and children, and via the web—we work to resource individuals and church communities in their Christian discipleship through the Bible, prayer and worship.

Our Barnabas children's team works with primary schools and churches to help children under 11, and the adults who work with them, to explore Christianity creatively and to bring the Bible alive.

To find out more about BRF and its core activities and ministries, visit:

www.brf.org.uk
www.brfonline.org.uk
www.biblereadingnotes.org.uk
www.barnabasinschools.org.uk
www.barnabasinchurches.org.uk
www.faithinhomes.org.uk
www.messychurch.org.uk
www.foundations21.net

If you have any questions about BRF and our work, please email us at

enquiries@brf.org.uk